A Simple and Easy way to GOD

And Other Heart-to-Heart Talks

J. P. Vaswani

Sterling Paperbacks

Books By J. P. Vaswani

In English:

The Seven Commandments of the Bhagavad Gita
Kill Fear Before Fear Kills You
Swallow Irritation Before Irritation Swallows You
Its All A Matter of Attitude
You Can Make A Difference
101 Stories For You and Me
108 Pearls of Practical Wisdom
108 Simple Prayers of A Simple Man
108 Thoughts on Success
114 Thoughts on Love
A Child of God
A Day with Dadaji
A Mystic of Modern India
Begin the Day with God
Beloved Dadaji
Conversations with Dadaji
Dada Answers
Daily Appointment With God
Daily Inspiration
Doors of Heaven
Education: What India Needs
Feast of Love
Five Fragrant Flowers
From Darkness Into Light
From Hell to Heaven
Glimpses
Glimpses Into Great Lives
God In Quest of Man
Hinduism
How to Have Real Fun Out of Life and other Talks
How to Make Your Life A Love Story
How to Overcome Temptations
How to Overcome Tensions
I Have Need of You
I Luv U, God!
Invest in the Child
Joy Peace Pills
Laugh Your Way to Health
Life After Death
Life is A Love Story
Love and Laugh!
Nestle Now
Notes from the Master's Lute
Pictures and Parables
Positive Power of Thanksgiving
Prayers of A Pilgrim
Prophets and Patriots
Sadhu Vaswani: His Life and Teachings
Little Lamps
Secrets of Health and Happiness
Shanti Speaks
Snacks for the Soul
More Snacks for the Soul
Stories for Meditation
Stories for You and Me
Teach Me to Pray
Tear-Drops (poems)
Temple Flowers
Ten Commandments of A Successful Marriage
The Holy Man of Hyderabad
The Kingdom of Krishna
A Little Book of Life
A Little Book of Wisdom
The Little Book of Prayer
The Little Book of Service
The Little Book of Success
The Little Book of Yoga
The Little Book of Freedom From Stress

The Magic of Forgiveness
The Simple Way
The Story of A Simple Man
The Way of *Abhyasa* (How to Meditate)
Ticket to Heaven
Twinkle, Twinkle Tiny Star
What You Would Like to Know about *Karma*
Whispers
Why Do Good People Suffer?
You Are Not Alone!
You Can Be A Smile Millionaire
Destination Happiness
Ladder of *Abhyasa*
Peace or Perish – There is no Other Choice
Good Parenting
Teachers Are Sculptors
I Am a Sindhi
The Perfect Relationship: *Guru and Disciple*
Sketches of Saints Known & Unknown
Short Sketches of Saints Known & Unknown
Management: Moment by Moment
Thus Have I Been Taught
Dewdrops of Love
A Treasure of Quotes
Living Legend
Saints for You and Me
Does God Have Favourites?
Nearer, My God, to Thee!
Many Paths: One Goal
Gateways to Heaven
New Education Can Make The World New
Saints With a Difference
What to do When Difficulties Strike
Shake Hands With Life

Recipe Books:
Delicious Vegetarian Recipes
Simply Vegetarian
90 Vegetarian Sindhi Recipes

In Hindi:
Ishwar Tujhe Pranaam
Prarthna Ki Shakti
Alwar Santon Ki Mahaan Gaathaayein
Atmik Jalpaan
Atmik Poshan
Bhale Logon Ke Saath Bura Kyon
Chitra Darshan
Dainik Prerna
Krodh Ko Jalayen, Swayam Ko Nahi
Mahan Purush Jeevan Darshan
Santon Ki Lila
Mrityun Hai Dwaar : Phir Kya?
Safal Vivah Ke Dus Rahasya
Jiski Jholi Main Hai Pyaar
Dar Se Mukti
Laghu Kathayein
Aapka Karm Aapka Bhagya Banate Hain

Books on Rev. Dada J. P. Vaswani
Legend of Love
Moments With A Master
Dada J. P. Vaswani: His Life & Teachings
A Pilgrim of Love
Dost Thou Keep Memory
Love Unlimited

STERLING PAPERBACKS
An imprint of
Sterling Publishers (P) Ltd.
A-59, Okhla Industrial Area, Phase-II, New Delhi-110020.
Tel: 26387070, 26386209; Fax: 91-11-26383788
E-mail: mail@sterlingpublishers.com
www.sterlingpublishers.com

A Simple and Easy Way to God
© 2011, J. P. Vaswani
ISBN 978 81 207 6006 6

All rights are reserved.
No part of this publication may be reproduced, stored in a retrieval system or transmitted, in any form or by any means, mechanical, photocopying, recording or otherwise, without prior written permission of the author.

DADA VASWANI BOOKS
Visit us online to purchase books on self improvement, spiritual advancement, meditation and philosophy. Plus audio cassettes, CDs, DVDs, monthly journals and books in Hindi.
www.dadavaswanisbooks.org

Printed in India
Printed and Published by Sterling Publishers Pvt. Ltd., New Delhi-110 020.

Contents

1. Let Faith Be Your Guide! 2
2. In Tune With Nature 15
3. Season Of Study 24
4. Pleasure Is Poison 33
5. Ten Marks Of A True Pilgrim 41
6. Why Do People Think Of Committing Suicide? 50
7. As You Think, So You Become! 59
8. The Choice Is Yours! 66
9. The Book Of The Heart Sufficeth! 75
10. The Easiest Way To Peace 85
11. Learn To Say, 'No'! 95
12. A Simple And Easy Way To God 106

13. Awareness Of God's Love 116
14. Unconditional Love 128
15. The Magic Of The Name Divine 140

More precious than the wealth of this world is faith in Him, who is too loving to punish, too wise to make a mistake.

Let Faith Be Your Guide!

I awoke this morning, with a prayer in my heart. I wanted God to grant me a special gift, a valuable blessing: the great gift of faith! I prayed to God that my faith may always remain solid as a rock, unshaken, unmoved by the vicissitudes of life and the ups and downs of fickle fortune.

A man may be affluent and possess enough material wealth to leave several of his future generations comfortable; he may be at the height of power, and enjoy unquestioned authority. But, let me tell you, if he lacks faith, his wealth and power are as nothing; indeed he is no better than a man afflicted with utter poverty – poverty of the Spirit! On the other hand, a man may possess nothing, he may not be anywhere near the higher echelons of power; he may not be wealthy; but if he has faith in God, then he is a master of himself, he is a king, who lacks nothing. A man of faith, I know, lives in stability and equanimity – the most enviable state of being!

It was a saint who often said, "Nothing in the morn have I, and nothing at night: yet there is none on earth, richer than I!"

What is it, you think, that made him so contented, so confident, so optimistic? The answer is simple: he was a man of faith! When you have faith in God, and your faith is solid as a rock – you need nothing, you feel yourself to be complete and contented in every respect, you feel secure and confident. Such a man does not worry, he does not fret and does not despair because his faith is always with him. He lives in that wonderful sense of security which comes from unshakeable faith in the Almighty.

The story is told to us of a saint, who sat in his *kutiya*, talking to his followers. It was a dark and stormy night. The *kutiya* was lit by a small earthenware lamp. All of a sudden, there was a sudden gust of wind which blew away the tiny flame of the earthenware lamp, plunging the *kutiya* in darkness. The *dervish* began to weep quietly. His devotees were shocked to see this, and they said to him, "Master! Pray do not worry, pray cease your weeping! We shall light the lamp in a moment and dispel the darkness. Please do not cry. Soon we shall have light in the *kutiya*."

It was done in a moment, as they had promised. The *dervish* looked at his devotees and they saw that his eyes were still tear-touched. He said to them, "When I saw the blast of the wind blow away the tiny flame, a thought came to my mind, 'What if the blast of desire blows away the flame of my faith? If my faith were extinguished? I would fall into a bottomless pit of darkness and despair'."

Rishis of our ancient India, time and again offered the immortal prayer, *"Tamaso Maa Jyotir Gamaya."* "O Lord, lead me out of darkness into Light." This light is the light of faith; this illumination which dispels the darkness is faith. The illumination has one message, "God, You are my protector, You are with me, You are watching me, You are watching over me." This faith of God's constant presence with him, illumines the soul of man.

What is faith? Faith is not blind, as some 'rationalists' would claim. Faith is *seeing* with the eyes of the heart. But alas, for many of us, the eyes of the heart are closed. When we open these eyes, we will see that all that has happened, has happened for the best, all that is happening is happening for the best, and all that will happen will happen for the best. There is a meaning of mercy in all that happens. God has a plan for everyone of us, and there is a Divine purpose in every little thing that happens to us. The great American poet, Whittier, said, "When faith is lost...the man is dead!"

Let me urge parents, "You must instill this kind of faith in your children." Let me also implore the teachers in the schools and the professors in the colleges, to sow the seeds of faith in their students. For faith is an invaluable treasure. It is the wealth that thieves cannot loot, and creditors cannot claim from you. Such a strong faith is what we all need today. Faith alone can give us true freedom – freedom from fear and all negative emotions.

Sometimes your biggest weakness can become your biggest strength. Take, for example, the story of this 10-year-old boy who decided to study judo despite the fact that he had lost his left arm in a devastating car accident.

An old Japanese judo master agreed to take him on as his pupil. The boy was earnest and sincere, and came for his lessons everyday. But he couldn't understand one thing: why, after three months of training, the master had taught him only one move, among the entire gamut of all judo moves.

"Sensei," the boy said to his master one day, "Shouldn't I be learning a few more moves?"

"This is the only move you know, but this is the only move you'll ever need to know," the Sensei replied.

The boy couldn't quite understand what this meant; but he had great faith in his teacher; so he kept on training with him.

Several months later, the Sensei took the boy to his first tournament. Surprising himself, the boy easily won his first two matches, using the one move that he had been taught. The third match proved to be a little more difficult, but after some time, his opponent became impatient and charged; the boy deftly used his one move to win the match. Still amazed by his success, the boy was now in the finals.

This time, his opponent was bigger, stronger, and more experienced. For a while, the boy appeared to be overmatched. Concerned that the boy might get hurt, the referee called a time-out. He was about to stop the match when the Sensei intervened.

"No," the Sensei insisted, "Let him continue."

Soon after the match resumed, his opponent made a critical mistake: he dropped his guard. Instantly, the boy used his one move to pin him down. The boy had won the match and the tournament. He was the champion!

On the way home, the boy and the Sensei reviewed every move in each and every match. Then the boy summoned the courage to ask what was really on his mind.

"Sensei, how did I win the tournament with only one move?"

"You won for two reasons," the Sensei answered. "First, you've almost mastered one of the most difficult throws in all of judo, for that was the one move I taught you. Second, the only known defence for that move is for your opponent to grab your left arm."

And of course, you and I know, that the boy did not have a left arm! The boy's biggest weakness had become his biggest strength! And he had capitalised on his faith to turn his weakness to his advantage.

We should never lose our faith in God, no matter how dark and hopeless things seem to be. An unforeseen, unpleasant or undesirable event should not shake our faith. Just as nature has its physical and subtle laws, so too, spiritual life also has certain principles. One such principle is faith. Great scientists like Newton and Einstein studied nature to give us its laws. Similarly, our saints and sages, who have studied the science of the Spirit, or *atma vidya*, have given us the laws of the Spirit. Faith links man with God. Faith brings peace and blessings. Faith can work miracles in life. Man does not have to climb a mountain peak, nor has he to wander in the forest, to discover the power of faith. Man can be linked with God, wherever he is, wherever he lives. All he has to do, is call out to the great Almighty and God responds immediately. When our bond with God is strong, we realise that God is our helper, our protector and our guardian and guide. Like Newton's Law of Gravitation, we have the Law of Faith. We gravitate towards His love, and His love does the rest. This Law works only when we surrender ourselves utterly and completely to God. And then, the experience of His greatness, His kindness and His benevolence becomes a part of our lives.

There is an amusing story about a group of men who came to a Saint of God. "O holy man, help us!" they pleaded. "Our village has been struck by a severe drought. We beg you to pray with us, so that God may send the rain down at once. We are sure it will pour if you join our prayers."

"When do you want to pray?" enquired the holy man.

"Right now," they answered. "Let us pray here and now. Let the Lord send down the rain forthwith."

The holy man said to them, "Where is your faith? You said you were sure that the Lord will answer our prayer; but where is the mark of that faith? Not one of you has brought an umbrella with you; not one of you has a raincoat. And yet you believe the rain will come down?"

It was Swami Vivekananda who said, "With His grace, we can cross the seven seas. But without His grace, we cannot even cross the threshold."

This is the kind of faith we need to sustain us through life.

Faith is necessary not only in crisis situations and emergencies, but also to battle the exhausting, crushing routine of everyday life.

There was a sister who was under tremendous pressure both at work and on the home front. The company she worked for was passing through a financial crisis, and was severely short-staffed, with each employee doing the work of two or three people. There was no question of complaining, because she knew she was lucky to have a job, while a dozen others like her had lost theirs. At home, she had an old mother to care for and a younger brother and sister to support. Sometimes, she said, she was overwhelmed by the thought of what lay ahead for her when she awoke in the morning.

I gave her a simple prayer. Every morning, as she awoke, I told her to hand her day over to the Lord and tell Him, "Lord, this day is Thine, and all the work I do, I offer to You. I know I cannot carry the load myself. I hand my life over to You. I beg You to get everything done for me."

She found a miraculous change in her life. Everything seemed to fall into place; her burdens seemed to lift of their own accord. Everything seemed, somehow, more manageable!

Believe that with God, all things are possible! Many doctors have assured us that they have seen men, after all therapy had failed, lifted out of affliction and disease by the serene effect of faith. Faith, indeed, seems to overcome even the so-called 'laws of nature'. And the occasions on which prayer has dramatically done this have been termed 'miracles'.

Are you one of those disgruntled people who feel that your life has had no miracles? Let me tell you, a constant, quiet miracle is taking place every day, every hour, every minute in the lives of men who have placed their trust in the Lord, and find His sustaining power flowing into their daily lives.

Therefore, trust in the Lord! In faith, you achieve harmony of body, mind and spirit which gives unshakeable strength to your weakest efforts. Did not Jesus say, "Ask and it shall be given to you?" True, prayer cannot bring the dead back to life, or wipe away pain and suffering. But prayer, like radium, is a source of luminous energy that can light up our lives.

As human beings, we seek to augment our finite energy by linking ourselves to God, who is the Source of infinite energy. His power is inexhaustible, and He is ready to give some of it to us so that we may do what we have to do. Just by asking for His help, our deficiencies are set right and we are restored, rejuvenated and strengthened.

We should build our lives in faith. We should sow the seeds of faith in children in their early childhood. This will help them to grow in faith and they will be able to meet the challenges of life with fortitude and faith.

The one lesson we all need to learn is – utter dependence on God! Everything else will follow. To surrender is to seek refuge, to trust in the Lord fully, completely, entirely. It is to know that He is the One Light that shines and shines and ever shines. Though the storms howl and the darkness grows deeper, His light shines on! He is the creator and the nourisher of all that is, He is the deliverer from whom all evils flee. He is nearer to us than our own heartbeats, and closer than our breathing. He is sufficient as a friend, sufficient as a helper. There is not a corner too remote for His help to reach us!

The night was dark and cloudy. Strange howls and eerie noises could be heard in the distance. Every rustle in the undergrowth sent a chill down one's spine. All alone, a weary traveller was crossing a thick forest.

"Keep moving as quickly as you can," he had been warned. "Be on your guard every second. Whatever you do, don't fall asleep, for the forest is full of man-eaters who will be out to get your blood."

The man was near the point of utter exhaustion. He felt he could not take a step further. He sank to the ground and prayed: "Lord, I cannot keep awake any longer. You are awake all the time. Is it necessary for both of us to be awake?"

So saying he fell into a deep slumber.

When he awoke, daylight was bright around him. It was long past dawn, and he saw a man standing guard next to him, armed with a gun.

"Who are you sir?" asked the traveller in surprise. "How is it that you are here in this obscure corner of the forest, patrolling the clearing where I have slept?"

"I was passing through the forest late last night, when I came upon you, sleeping soundly," the stranger replied. "It seemed to me that you, perhaps, were unaware of the danger of this place. So I decided to stop here and keep watch while you slept!"

"All gratitude to God!" exclaimed the traveller. "How true it is that He guides us and guards us wherever we are, whatever we do!"

Walk with God today and trust Him for the morrow! This is the priceless secret of true peace and lasting joy. Faith and trust are the twin powers that can banish worry from your life. This is not blind faith that I'm talking about – it is strong, reasoned, well-founded faith in God's goodness and care. It is the positive power that enables you to stand up and fight, and overcome your problems successfully. Remember, I said,

'*Walk* with God'; *not* 'Sit back and wait for God to do something'!

Lazy people cannot draw to themselves God's help! But if you put in your best efforts and leave the rest to the Lord, I'm sure He will fulfill his part of the deal.

When you place your trust in the Lord, when you surrender utterly and completely to His Divine Will, you will find wonderful things happen in your life! Here is a Zen story which illustrates this truth.

There was a disciple, who was asking his master about developing the right attitude to life and work.

"How can I acquire discipline in my search for truth?"

"You must exercise yourself."

"How may I exercise myself?"

"You must eat when you are hungry; you must sleep when you are tired."

"But..." the disciple stammered. "That's what everyone does. Do you mean to say that is sufficient to exercise oneself to acquire discipline?"

"But that is exactly what most people do *not* do!" the master asserted. "When they eat, they are worrying about one hundred things. When they sleep, they dream of one thousand things. This is not at all the kind of exercise I meant!"

The Zen master in fact, had uttered a great truth! Most of us are unable to engage ourselves fully even in the routine tasks of everyday life. The reason? *We do not live in the present.* We are drowning in the regrets and disappointments of the past – or losing our balance in vague imaginative anxieties about the future. What we fail to realise is that life would be so much more satisfying and meaningful, and we ourselves would be happier and more peaceful if we learn to live in the present – walking with God today and trusting Him for the morrow!

When you feel that He is taking care of your needs, you cease to worry! You do not have to plan in advance for unforeseen eventualities. You do not have to worry about calamities. You simply allow the Divine Plan to unfold. You claim nothing; you ask nothing; you seek nothing; you plan nothing. You simply become a channel for the Divine Plan to flow through.

How many of us are capable of such faith and trust?

Nature is truly the environment of the *atman*, the eternal soul within each human being.

In Tune With Nature

The incident that I am about to narrate to you happened a long, long time ago. It was a hot, blistering summer day. Gurudev Sadhu Vaswani was in Rameshwaram, a sacred pilgrimage centre in South India. He was a well-known and highly respected spiritual leader in the South; some of his earliest books had been published in Madras. He would have been accorded the formal welcome due to a visiting dignitary at Rameshwaram, if he had chosen to announce his plans. But, that was not his way! He had requested the devotees travelling with him, not to disclose his identity. He said, "I wish to visit this sacred place as a simple man, a simple pilgrim."

Many of you may know that Rameshwaram is famous for its monumental temple. It is said that this is where Sita and Sri Rama worshipped Lord Shiva and offered their gratitude to Him, on their triumphant return from Lanka. In later times, the Hindu kings of the region built a huge temple here to commemorate this great event. It is a temple with stunning architecture, with huge *parikramas,* large courtyards, and a central pyramidal structure containing the main sanctum sanctorum. The temple also has what is perhaps the longest corridor of the medieval world, measuring over 4000 feet.

It was with great reverence and devotion that Gurudev Sadhu Vaswani went to visit this temple. But, alas! What he saw there, hurt him deeply. In one sanctum, a priest was offering worship. He was holding a small metal bell in one hand, rattling it fervently, and was collecting the money for the deity with the other hand. Those who did not give him any money, were barred from entering the sanctum sanctorum. When Gurudev Sadhu Vaswani saw this, his eyes were touched with tears. He could not bear this gross commercialisation of the temple worship.

In the evening, he again visited the temple, to join in the prayerful *aarti* – the worship offered at the sacred hour of sunset. The priest, performing the *aarti*, asked Gurudev Sadhu Vaswani, to put a rupee coin in the *aarti thali*. Gurudev Sadhu Vaswani smiled and put a copper coin in the plate. This enraged the priest so much that he flung the plate at him!

Gurudev Sadhu Vaswani was an angel of compassion. He smiled at the priest and in his ever-sweet voice said to him, "I pray that you do not worship money but worship Sri Rama, Who resides within you. I pray that you do not worship the idol in this stone temple, but worship the true Sri Rama, Whose temple is enshrined within your heart. The truest worship is the prayer of the soul. In fact, every heart, every little creation is a paean of praise to Him, to His splendour! I only beg you to remember this: that the entire creation is an offering unto Him. The entire universe is a divine prayer. Day in and day out, creation offers worship to Him, to the Perfect Creator. And no money is ever demanded of us if we wish to join this prayer!"

Those of us who accompanied him, did not quite understand what he meant. We asked him, "Please explain to us master, how is it that the universe offers worship to God?" Gurudev Sadhu Vaswani smiled and explained, "God is being worshipped, by the leaves in the trees, by the song of the birds, by the flowing waters of the rivers, by the fragrance of the flowers that bloom, by the gentle wafting of the cool breeze that blows around us! Let us join in this universal worship, which is an experience of feeling divinity in every single aspect of creation."

Everywhere the flowers bloom; everywhere the stars shine; everywhere the wind blows; everywhere the waves rise and roll; everywhere the divine prayer is sung. "Come dear ones, come and join this universal prayer to Him. This prayer is Eternal; this prayer is timeless." These words are addressed to all of us. They are addressed to me and many of you. 'Build your life in Truth and Love, and you will be able to experience this Divine revelation'.

Five hundred years ago, Guru Nanak gave the same teaching at the Jagannath Temple, in Puri, Orrisa. The priest there was offering worship, *aarti* – the plate of worship was made of gold, it was studded with pearls and expensive jewels. The lamp was lit. The bells were ringing, drums were beating and the devotees were standing in reverence before the deity. But there were two men, who were unmindful of everything around, and were sitting on the floor, a little away from the worshippers, paying no heed to what was going on. Noticing this, the priest performing the *aarti* was upset. After the *aarti* was over, he admonished the two devotees sitting on the floor! "How can you be so irreverent? You have insulted God by not standing and offering worship during the *aarti*!"

The two men thus admonished were none other than Guru Nanak and his dear disciple, Mardana.

Guru Nanak greeted the angry outburst of the priest with a gentle glance. He humbly said, "I too, was offering worship to God." The priest sneered at him. "What kind of worship is this? Where is the lamp? Where are the flowers? Where is the sandalwood paste? And you say you were performing worship!"

Guru Nanak, in reply to the query of this ignorant man, sang the *aarti* from his heart.

Gagan mein thal,
Rav chand deepak bane,
Tarka mandal janak moti...

What a profound teaching the great Guru conveys to us through this *aarti*! Guru Nanak explains,

"The sky is the plate, with millions of jewelled stars;

The bright lamps – the sun and moon shine eternally!"

Isn't this the worship of God? Nature, with its five elements, bears eternal testimony to the power of the Creator. This worship offered in the Temple of Nature is ceaseless, ongoing, permanent. It is not restricted by time; it is not confined to sunrise, sunset or mid-day. As for our temples, we worship there at select timings; the *pujas* and rituals are at specific times; people go there whenever it is convenient for them. Man worships God once or twice a day. His *aarti* is limited to morning and evening. But the flowers, rivulets, the winds, the trees, the birds, the sun, the moon and the stars are a perpetual prayer to the Almighty.

We are so fortunate, that we live in this Temple of Nature. Let our entire life be an offering, a worship to the Lord! Every moment of our life should be dedicated to God! Every moment of our life, should make us aware of our Creator! We should be aware of His presence and of His kindness! This is true worship!

This awareness will transform our lives. This awareness will wean us away from every act of violence; from flesh-food; from alcohol; from every evil. All we have to do is be in tune with Nature to create such awareness.

In the dark of the night, the moon sheds its silvery beams on us, as if saying, "Open your eyes, look at the beautiful worship being offered to God!" As the multicoloured hues of blooming flowers captivate our eyes, they too, tell us, "Join us in offering praise and thanks to God!" But we do not respond, because we are not yet 'in synch', in tune with Nature. Remember, each one of us is an integral part of the universe. We are the rightful priests, the ordained residents of this Temple of Nature. But we have alienated ourselves from Nature. Man, in his ignorance, desires to conquer Nature, conquer Space. In his vanity and pride, man even thinks himself to be superior to Nature. Man has walked on the moon; man wants to explore other planets. But let me tell you, even if man walks over the moon, and his rockets go traveling to the other planets, he will still not be a conqueror. He is only a wanderer, a lonely explorer, who is trying to discover the many wonders, the many secrets of God's creation. For the universe we live in, is only one of the many universes created by God. The earth we inhabit, is only one of the thousands of planets in our Universe. Our earth is like a grain of sand, in the limitless ocean of the Universes. Then let us just consider, how insignificant, how pathetically small we are in the entire scheme of creation! And yet, we regard ourselves as great beings, as the crown of creation!

Man is a part of nature. Therefore, he should live in harmony with nature. That is the way to happiness.

This rhythm, this attempt to be 'in tune' with nature, will still the mind and bring tranquility which is born of harmony. The whole universe is holy. It is a Divine Prayer that is being offered to God, at every moment, every living second. Join in that holy prayer and a time will come, when you would want to merge with it. All you have to do, to participate in this universal prayer, is to keep your thoughts pure, keep a constant watch over yourself. May you be ever vigilant, ever watchful, that you do not disregard the laws of nature!

Nature is absorbed in the worship of the One Creator, the One Lord of all that is. It is scientifically proved that everything in nature emits light. Nature is spreading light with the message, 'Kindle the Light in your heart'.

What kind of light should you kindle in your heart? The light of Love Divine. Therefore, sing the Name Divine. Spread the Light of faith and devotion all around you. Let this light spread far and wide, like the fragrance of everything in Nature; let this light emanate from your heart, like the light emitted by flowers, leaves and trees. Be pure and selfless like Nature. Let your pure love fill the world with its fragrance. If you too, want to spread this fragrance all around you, then bear witness to the truth. Truth has fragrance. Truth has simplicity. Truth has serenity. Of what use is affluence and wealth built upon untruth? It will only give out the foul smell of rotten garbage within.

Nature is created from the Eternal Truth. Align yourself with nature. Gaze upon the stars; feel the gentle sway of the breeze; watch the wind dance its way through the grass; sit on the banks of a river and meditate on its beautiful flow. View the cascades over the hills; marvel at the mountains; stand on the vast sandy expanses of the seashore, and be mesmerized by the ceaseless motion of the dark and deep blue waves. And you will hear Nature sing to you:

> Make your life a hymn
> Make your life a lyric of love.

Nature's message is simple – remain in balance, be in harmony. Be in harmony with yourself, with your surroundings, with nature and with the entire universe. We all vibrate to each other's 'Light' vibrations. Our thoughts and our emotions are all linked to the centre of Oneness. Any evil thought, any base emotion will disturb the harmony in the Universe. It will ultimately create unhappiness for us, as well as for others. Therefore, let us build our life on Truth. Let us be pure in thought, word and deed. Let us be in tune with nature. Let us always bear in mind the essence of nature's message to us: which is, to give, give and give, without any thought of return. To give in silence. To offer all that we have, and all that we are, in service and sacrifice. To become worthy participants in the Eternal Prayer of creation!

The mind needs to be cleansed of the clutter of accumulated negative thoughts and pressures. Meditation empties the mind and energises the nervous system. Life without meditation is empty as the desert-sands. It is very much like a well without water, a garden without flowers, a temple without a light.

Season Of Study

Every year in India, on the full moon day of the month of *Ashad*, according to the Hindu calendar, we observe with great solemnity and fervour, the sacred day of Guru Poornima. It is a day when we rededicate ourselves to the Guru. This day is of great significance in the Hindu calendar for geographical and climatic reasons too; for it marks the beginning of what is called *Chaturmaas* – the four months of rain and wind, which our holy ones, saints and *sannyasis* habitually dedicate to austerity, fasts, worship and prayers. *Acharyas* and *sannyasis* usually do not travel during these four months. But *chaturmaas* is equally significant for all of us. Spiritually, it is regarded as the season for *Abhyas* – the study of self growth.

What is so special about this season? During these four months, the Cosmic Energy of the Universe is conducive to the *sadhak* or seeker, on his spiritual path. During these four months, the dedicated *sadhak* does not travel, nor does he wander, but stays in one place and focuses on the study of the Knowledge of Truth. As a seeker, he uses these four months, not merely to study and learn, but to put into practice the knowledge he has painstakingly gathered from the lives of the saints, from his reading of the scriptures and his association with the holy ones. For we must realise, being physically present in the *satsang*, hearing discourses regularly, or the mechanical reading and recitation of the scriptures, is not sufficient to help us realise the Truth. On the contrary, it is so much empty 'knowledge' which merely adds to the burden of our intellect – and, if we are not careful, this load can crush man under its weight.

A story in one of the Upanishads compares such knowledge to a donkey carrying invaluable treasure of sandalwood. The donkey does not know the worth of the treasure on his back. He is only aware of the load on his back, which is heavy and unbearable. A *sadhak* with all his knowledge is like that, aware only of the burden he carries, but unable to put it to good use.

The *Chaturmaas* – 'four months' are meant to help us realise the true value of the treasure of pure sandalwood that many of us carry in vain – the fragrant sandalwood of True Knowledge.

Sri Ramakrishna Paramhansa would often tell his disciples, that there is no magic in turning milk into ghee. If you want ghee, (as every housewife in those days would tell you) you have to go through the process of making ghee. First you have to boil the milk, then remove the cream, store the cream and make it into curd, then separate out its 'whey', churn the solid into butter and then melt it to get ghee. The same is true of an aspirant. He has to put in his own effort and go through a process. The 'bliss' is to be earned. There is no magic wand, or magic formula, which will bring it to you 'in an instant'.

The same is true of 'blessings'. The blessings of a saint or a holy One, are to be earned and earned the hard way. By merely calling out, "Bless me, bless me", you will not be showered with the blessings you seek. Let me say to you, even to get the blessings of a saint's glance, you have to work hard – through devotion, humility and service. And we have a season which is meant for us to practice these virtues – *Chaturmaas.* These four months are truly invaluable. It is up to us to put them to the best possible use.

Gurudev Sadhu Vaswani urged us to study and follow the norms and the spiritual regimen strictly. He said,

> By merely jumping into the ocean
> You do not get oysters with pearls:
> Dive deep into the ocean,
> Dive tirelessly and you will find,
> The invaluable treasure of pearls that you seek.

Ask any pearl-diver, and he will tell you that in order to dive deep, you have to take the requisite training. You have to learn swimming; you have to acquire the special skill of diving underwater; and you have to develop an eye for the oysters with pearls! You have to go through a long and tedious learning process, before you can even spot, leave alone lay your hands, on a pearl!

Is this not true of all human endeavours? How does a toddler learn to walk? At first he just crawls; then he takes a few steps with support, then he steadies himself and learns to walk and finally learns to run. During this learning process, the child stumbles and falls, often bruising and hurting himself, before he is able to acquire the skill of walking steadily and straight.

Our studies in school go through the same process. We learn to write, beginning with just vertical lines drawn up and down, then little circles and semi-circles, and then come the actual words of the alphabet. We have to repeat each line, each dot, each circle, umpteen times, till the teacher is pleased with the formations and we are able to write even the simple ABCD. We have to practice the art of copy writing, as it used to be called in my days, for at least two years to reach even this preliminary stage of schooling.

Practice, as we know, makes a man perfect. We bear witness to this truth in our daily life. For a toddler, it is a guided struggle to learn walking; for a child, it is a guided practice to learn to write ABCD. For those on the spiritual path too, the same holds good. Have you ever watched a woman walk on a rope? In rural Maharashtra, this scene is very common. Not just men or women, but even small children keep balance with a stick and walk on a tight rope, high above the ground, tied to poles at both ends. This spectacle of acrobats against the background of beating drums is amazing. Their ability to balance on the rope, is truly astounding. It is nothing but hard work and regular practice which makes them perform these dangerous acts, so skillfully. I am certain that they must have fallen several times, even hurt themselves badly, during their early practice sessions. But their perseverance and continuous practice makes them learn the art of tightrope walking till they are experts at it!

That reminds me of a story. A wealthy businessman was about to enrol his son in a famous university. But he was taken aback when he realised that it would be four years before the boy would be granted his basic degree; and in between, there would be eight semesters with mid-term tests, assignments and exams at the end of each.

Frowning, he flipped through the catalogue of courses and demanded of the Dean, "Why does my son have to go through so many courses? Can't you make the whole thing shorter? I want him to get out of it quickly!"

"Certainly, he can take a shorter course," replied the Dean politely. "It all depends on what he wants to make of himself. You see, it takes 20 – 30 years for an oak tree to grow; but a mushroom springs up overnight."

We are all attracted by short-cuts, quick fixes and easy solutions. But, like the oak tree, the mind and character take time to shape up and grow. And we require all eternity to attain to perfection! And there are no short cuts on this path!

This journey on the path of *abhyasa* is difficult. There are pebbles and stones and thorns on the way; there are hills and dales to cross tunnels to pass through – there is 'the dark night of the soul' to go through.

Do not despair at the hurdles on this journey! Let me assure you, that at the end of the tunnel is the light; after the strenuous climb, there is the peak of panoramic view. So do not give in to despair, if you fall and hurt yourself. Sri Krishna says, 'O Arjuna, none of your efforts are wasted."

Nothing in this universe goes waste. Every effort brings its reward. Hence do not despair. Put in your effort and see the magic happen! Gurudev Sadhu Vaswani has outlined for us, the regimen to be followed on this path.

The first discipline to be observed is *naam simran*, chanting the Name Divine.
The second discipline is *dhyaan* or meditation.
The third discipline is *kirtan*, singing the glories of the Lord!
The fourth discipline is prayer with devotion.
The fifth discipline is service to mankind.

Chanting the Name Divine, cleanses us of all 'interior' filth and ugliness. It takes away the negativity that is deep within us. Meditation creates inner spaces into which we might recede and receive Divine vibrations. *Kirtan* helps us to bond with the Cosmic Divine Energy. It attracts Divine Light, because praising the Lord, singing His glories is a way of acknowledging His Presence. Prayer too, is a form of connectivity. It links you with the Divine Source. Selfless service, performed in humility, is the purpose of this human birth, and it is our bounden duty to see that it is fulfilled. As Gurudev Sadhu Vaswani has said, "Service of the poor is worship of God."

It is true, there are difficulties in following these five disciplines. But, I repeat, there is no need to give in to despair. Give yourself time. For example, chanting the Name Divine is a cleansing process, but a slow one. Meditation too, is difficult, as the nature of this human mind is to wander in many directions. Hence, choose the image of a holy one, and try to meditate on that physical object. Slowly the physical object will fade away, leaving the Divine Cosmic space, and you will learn to meditate on the Abstract Invisible Infinite! Meditation, as I have stressed repeatedly, is best done at the *Brahma Mahurat* – early dawn. Just try to meditate early in the morning, for a week, and you will be amazed at the change within you!

Interior cleansing through these disciplines – *naam simran, dhyaan*, prayer, *kirtan*, and *seva* – is essential, for we cannot offer God, a dirty, polluted heart. We have to create a beautiful temple, where we can invite Him to reside! Once the cleansing and purification are accomplished, all you have to do is call upon God, with deep devotion and yearning, promising Him that you will serve Him with dedication – by serving His myriad broken images, the poor and the forlorn of this earth. When you call upon Him, in this state of mind, He will willingly step in and occupy the throne of your heart, and you will experience the Divine Bliss, that the seekers of this ancient land have sought from time immemorial.

We think it is we who enjoy pleasures. But, in truth, it is pleasures that enjoy us. For while pleasure always remains young and vital, it is we who keep growing old, getting consumed in the fire of pleasure.

Pleasure Is Poison

Satsang has a positive effect on man. *Satsang* creates pure and positive vibrations which neutralise the negative emotions of man. When we go to *satsang*, we get to hear discourses of holy men, participate in the recitation of sacred scriptures and singing of soulful *bhajans*. All of this helps to raise the level of positive vibrations which energise us. For a short time at least, we forget our mundane worries and get immersed in the pure waters of the Spirit. Our emotions rise above the senses, and we cry out, "O Lord! This is bliss. O Lord! You have given me this beautiful gift of life. Until now I have wasted it. But from now onwards, I will strive to achieve the goal of this human birth!"

Unfortunately for us, these emotions of sublimity do not last long. The moment we leave the *satsang*, we are submerged in worldly concerns. We are drawn into the vicious circle of worry, anxiety, envy and jealousy. We are pulled back into the quicksand of pleasures and wrong doing. We are lost in negativity. Dark clouds surround us and we are back where we started. What is the reason? Why could we not sustain those positive energies a little longer? Why is our spiritual effort so short lived?

The reason is simple. Our senses are constantly running after the pleasures of life. But, as the poet John Keats pointed out so perceptively, pleasure and pain are very close to each other: in fact, they are two sides of the same coin.

> ...and aching Pleasure nigh,
> Turning to poison while the bee-mouth sips...

Just consider those phrases; *aching pleasure*; *turning to poison*; even while it is being sipped. Does the poem not say it all? Pleasures bind us, imprison us and ultimately bring us the pain of despair and frustration. Pleasure is poison. Sooner or later, it shows its effect. It destroys man. It kills man.

Man's pleasure hunting is a continuous activity. The senses run constantly, chasing one pleasure after another. Each pleasure leaves us feeling unsatisfied; we feel that something is missing; something is lacking; may be we should try something else? And this game of the senses continues without a respite, leaving man with the burden of emptiness and negativity. But is this man's natural condition? Are we doomed to be forever empty, forever unhappy and unfulfilled?

The answer is 'No'! Man is an incarnation of *shakti*. Man is a finite part of the Infinite. It is his birthright to be happy and at peace with himself. Man has pure positive energy, which needs to be released.

Satsang is one such way of releasing the positive energy to put us on the path of bliss.

The Katha Upanishad tells us of the young boy Nachiketa, who is granted a boon by Yamaraj. He enquires of the Lord of Death, "Pray teach me how men may be freed from this terrible, crushing burden of the cycle of birth and death!"

Yamaraj is taken aback. "You have asked a very difficult question," he explains to the boy. "Even the *Devatas* do not know of this way. Even the Gods have quarreled over the issue. It is abstruse and complex, and you are very young. Ask for something else instead, and I will happily grant it to you. Land, cows, horses, elephants, gold, silver, the kingdoms of the earth, whatever you ask I shall give you — ask for wealth and a long life, sons and grandsons. It will all be granted to you. Beautiful girls will be in your service, who will sing songs for you, and fill your life with pleasure. I will give you everything, but do not ask me to give you an answer to this question."

Nachiketa tells him, "I could of course ask you for land, cows, elephants, all the pleasures and the wealth of this world — but Lord, you know and I know, these are ephemeral, they are but passing pleasures. They may be mine today, but gone tomorrow. How can I call them mine? I seek from you that treasure, the treasure of truth, which is truly lasting; and who better than you, the Lord of death, to give me the right answer to this question?"

This young boy had the good sense, the will power not to be lured by the pleasures of this world. Alas, how many of us have that courage and conviction?

The Bhagavad Gita describes the world as 'ephemeral' i.e. temporary and 'without happiness' i.e. an ocean of misery. As I mentioned earlier, 'pleasures' turn into 'poison' here. When man is caught in the toil of evil pleasures, it squeezes him to a painful death.

Let me repeat the beautiful fable which I have often narrated to you, if only to refresh your memory. When the universe was created, the Supreme Creator gave every living being its share of happiness. But man, with his vicious mind, misused it. The Supreme Creator was unhappy. He called the Angels from the *swargaloka* and asked them to suggest a solution.

One Angel said, "Bury happiness in the depth of the ocean." Brahma, the Supreme Creator, did not accept it. He said, "Man will dive deep and fish out happiness from the bottom of sea."

Another Angel suggested, "Bury happiness in the deep interiors of the earth." To this, Brahma replied, "Man will dig the earth and bring out happiness."

There were many suggestions, but none appealed to Brahma. At last, He gave the verdict, "Bury happiness in a place, where man cannot find it. And that place is within his own heart. Man will run after worldly pleasures; he will run after the mirage. The happiness within him would be covered by so many veils of

Maya, that no ordinary man would be able to lift them, leave alone seek to find happiness within."

Since then, man, like the proverbial musk-deer, has been running after the fragrance of truth, when the fragrance of truth is within him, in his heart! *Satsang* helps us to stop running outside of 'ourselves'. It barricades us against (may be I should say, protects us from) the external pleasures of the world. It helps us to go within, for there lies the Eternal Bliss we so desperately seek.

The Shrimad Bhagavatam contains many stories and tales of wisdom. One of them is about Raja Yayati. He was what we would call a hedonist — an absolute pleasure seeker. He had enjoyed his life to the core. When he grew old, his senses dimmed and his body became weak, and he could no longer enjoy the physical pleasures of life. Yet, his desires were aflame, and he yearned to enjoy more and more pleasure.

He was advised that if he were able to borrow youth from someone, he would once again be able to enjoy his life to the hilt. Let me explain what this meant: if someone agreed to give him their youth, zest and energy and accept his old age with its weakness and frailty, then he would be able to indulge in all the pleasures that he craved for. But who on earth would consent to such an exchange?

Raja Yayati was determined to give it a try. He went to his eldest son, with the request to give him his youth. The son refused him. "How can I give you my youth? Do I not have the right to enjoy my life? You have had your turn, and you cannot ask for mine now!"

Raja Yayati went to his second son. He was refused in the same way. He then approached his third, fourth and the fifth son. They were not willing to part with their youth for the sake of gratifying their ageing father. However the youngest son, out of love, and duty agreed to give his youth to his father.

Raja Yayati, now rejuvenated, began his pleasure hunt. But his appetite could not be appeased. A time came, when he realised the futility of the superficial life of pleasures. He realised that these pleasures were but temporary. Disgusted, and wiser with experience, he returned the youth of his son and sought out a better life, suited to his old age.

Gautama Buddha was no sensualist. But he too, was disillusioned with the luxuries of life. He gave up his princely palace and future kingship. He went out in search of truth.

We all, in our own way, realise at some stage or the other, that worldly pleasures and material comforts cannot really give us the joy we seek. We learn the harsh lesson that pleasure and pain go hand in hand. It is the unbearable pain of this realisation that brings us to the stage of *vairagya*, or detachment from the senses. And then, we cease running after pleasures, and venture in search of solace, peace and true happiness. And that is a long journey!

Look at the Yon tree, it is bound to the earth yet it seeks the sky.

Ten Marks Of A True Pilgrim

Pilgrims are we all upon this earth. For this earth is not our true home. It is only a bridge across which we must traverse to get across to the other shore, where lies our true destination. But the fact of the matter is we are so caught up in the Vanity Fair that is the world, that we have lost awareness of our true being. We have become unconscious of the truth of life. We seem to live in a state of spiritual slumber.

The message of Gurudev Sadhu Vaswani was: *Jago, Jago* ! "Awake, awake, and do not fall aslumber."

Once Gurudev Sadhu Vaswani was asked a question, "Who are you?" In reply he said, "I am a peasant, I am a farmer. I keep on moving from place to place sowing seeds in aspiring hearts."

What kind of seeds are those? They are the seeds of love, purity, truth and simplicity.

Gurudev Sadhu Vaswani awakened us by pointing out to us that we were like alien birds here upon this earth. "This is not your homeland," he repeated to us, constantly. "Your true home is where you came from – your native land."

Today, people spend millions of rupees on building homes and furnishing them. They think, "This is my home. This is my abode. Let me make it as comfortable, as luxurious as I can." What they fail to realise is that this world itself, is only a travellers' inn, where people come, rest for a while and go away. To use a modern metaphor, this world is like the arrival and departure lounge in an airport! In Gurudev's words, "Pilgrims are ye all. Our pilgrimage is to the eternal, where is our home."

How can we ensure that as pilgrims, we are on the right path? What are the practices and procedures we may adopt to ensure that we are prepared for the pilgrimage to the other shore? From time immemorial, our ancestors have adopted many such practices and procedures, which may be helpful to us. One of these is to set aside certain days of the month to remind ourselves of who we are, where we come from, and whence are we moving.

In India, the eleventh day after the *Poornima* (full moon) and *Amavasya* (new moon) is called *Ekadashi*. There are two such days per month, one each in the bright and dark half of the month. *Ekadashi* is known as a sacred day. It is believed that our negative karmas are neutralised, if we undertake fasting, prayer and meditation on this day.

Gurudev was born on an *Ekadashi Day*, in the month of November 1879. Hence, all of us at the Sadhu Vaswani Mission observe *Ekadashi* as a doubly sacred day. For many of us, it is a day of fasting, prayer and dedication.

What is the significance of fasting on such days? Choosing to refrain from food is a physical, mental and spiritual discipline, *tapas*, that helps us overcome addictive behavioural patterns and bad habits. The Sanskrit word for fast is '*upa-vaas*', which means staying close to God. The original concept of fasting entailed a deviation, a departure from the routine lifestyle and devoting one day to introspection, reflection and meditation. The person who fasted was supposed to distance himself from his appetite and his senses, from the petty concerns of worldly life and think only about God. As any indulgence in worldly pleasure would deviate from this pursuit, he followed a simple routine on this day. Thus rich, *rajasic* food was avoided and a simple diet was taken to sustain the body. The intention was neither to starve the body nor to indulge it.

There are certain days that Hindus set apart for spiritual quietude and meditation. The idea is to refrain from routine worldly pursuits, and enter into nurturing activities like meditation, recitation from the scriptures, etc. Many devotees seek the company of 'mindful' friends, by attending *satsang*. Above all, *Ekadashi* is an individual expression. The observances can vary from person to person.

But the true significance of *Ekadashi* is not in the special food that is eaten; there are men and women who fast on *Ekadashi* day but eat a rich diet of dry fruits, nuts and fresh fruits. And then just to pass away their time, they go to a cinema or a club. The true meaning of fasting is to develop the self control to eat as little as possible and to spend time in meditation or solitude. The true meaning of fasting is to devote time and energy to the worship of the Lord. Fasting regularly on *Ekadashi* day has two main advantages. Firstly, it is good for your health; and secondly, it is thought to give premonition about one's death. The faithful ones believe that pious people who regularly fast on *Ekadashi* day come to know when and how death will come to them. This only goes to show that *Ekadashi* is a very holy day, especially, the *Prabodhini Ekadashi*. This Ekadashi brings the message of self enquiry in solitude. Self enquiry is the beginning of a mystical journey.

What are the marks of a pilgrim on the mystic path?

1. A pilgrim loves one and all.

His love is universal and unconditional. It is love without any attachments. This is the best kind of love that a human being is capable of; it is the true art of living. From a practical point of view, you should love your near and dear ones, your children, your parents and other family members. But let this love be a duty, and not lead to an attachment! A pilgrim's heart is filled with an abundance of love. But he is not attached to anyone, he is not attached to any object or any being.

Fulfil your obligations, do your duty, give the love of your heart to all around you, but be detached in the heart within. No one belongs to you! You belong entirely and wholly to the Lord.

2. A pilgrim's thoughts are clear.

His speech is pure. His actions are pure. The Lord tells us in the Bhagavad Gita, that those actions and words that cause harm and pain to others must be avoided. Therefore, the pilgrim must say and do what is true, what is good for everyone, and what is not injurious to any living being.

3. A pilgrim walks the path of truth.

We often speak lies and that is the root of all sin and suffering. *Satyam vada, krodam ma kuru* is the very first lesson of spiritual life, and an essential mark of the pilgrim. He always speaks the truth; he is always true to his higher self.

4. A pilgrim keeps himself away from all gossip and controversies.

He does not criticise anyone nor does he hear any complaints and criticism from others. Once a devotee came to Gurudev Sadhu Vaswani and said, "My mind wanders when I sit to meditate." Gurudev Sadhu Vaswani asked him, "Do you criticise anyone?" The devotee replied, "No. I do not criticise anyone nor do I degrade anyone." Gurudev Sadhu Vaswani then asked him, "Do you hear the gossip criticising others?" The devotee replied, "Yes. I do listen to the criticism of others." Gurudev Sadhu Vaswani said, "Even if you do not criticise anyone, but hear others' criticism, you become a passive participant in gossip."

A true pilgrim keeps himself away from all unpleasant, unproductive talk.

5. A pilgrim realises the Oneness of all creation.

Once a saint gave his disciples the teaching: "Do not become a pair of scissors, but be like a needle." The disciples were puzzled; they asked the saint to elucidate the point. The saint said, "The needle sews clothes, stitches up tears and cuts in the fabric. But the scissor cuts the cloth asunder. Hence, wherever you go, be like the needle and patch up differences; sew up tears and cuts; bring people together. Bind them in the silken thread of your love, because in reality we all are one!"

On the spiritual plane we all are one. There is no difference between you and me. In the physical world we find everyone different and hence we behave selfishly. We all are one. Hence we have a moral responsibility towards everyone of our fellow human beings, every being that breathes the breath of life. Our conduct should be ethical. There are people who think of their profits only, they do not care about others' welfare. The only motive of their life is to earn higher profits. These men are like scissors.

6. A pilgrim is an epitome of compassion.

His compassion moves out not only to men but also to birds and animals. He does not eat flesh-food, because to him animals are as dear as human beings.

7. A pilgrim always speaks gently.

He speaks sweetly. Everyone of us has a choice, either to speak harshly or to speak gently. We should always speak gently and sweetly.

Sant Gyaneshwar once said to his disciples, "When you get up from your sleep in the morning, regard it as the last day of your life."

Once we realise that we have only twenty-four hours left we would try to be as good as possible, to do as much good as possible. We would try to be sweet and gentle and helpful.

8. A pilgrim chants the Name Divine.

The Name of God is a great purifier and the purification is the very first step on the mystic path.

9. A pilgrim meditates on God everyday.

He does not miss his daily appointment with God. Fix a time for your meditation. Resolve that you will meditate for fifteen minutes or half an hour or an hour everyday. During this period you can chant the Name Divine, you can commune with God, meditate on some inspirational teachings, or pick up a sentence from a scripture and reflect on it.

10. A pilgrim prays for the Universe.

His prayer is, "All men, all birds and all animals, all living and non-living things, may they all, without exception be happy and full of bliss and peace."

These are the ten marks of the pilgrim on the mystic path.

Pick up any of these attributes for self growth and improvement. Practise at least one of them to perfection. Your pilgrimage to the Eternal will be richly blessed.

The truth is, there is no problem that does not have a solution. The man with the positive attitude thinks of the solution – while the man with the negative attitude only thinks of the problem. We need people who bring solutions to problems, not problems to solutions.

Why Do People Think Of Committing Suicide?

Optimism is defined as "an inclination to put the most favourable construction upon actions and events or to anticipate their best possible outcome". It is thought to be the philosophical opposite of pessimism. Pessimism, derived from the Latin root, *pessimus* (worst), is a state of mind which makes our perception of life negative, especially with regard to future events. Optimists generally believe that people and events are inherently good, so that most situations work out in the end for the best. Pessimism, on the other hand, is sometimes thought to be a negative self-fulfilling prophecy; that if an individual feels that something is bad, it is likely to get worse! Oscar Wilde defined a pessimist thus: "One who, when he has the choice of two evils, chooses both."

I was reminded of this definition recently, when I received a letter through courier. The letter had been sent by a lady living abroad. The letter read, "What I'm going to do is against the teachings of Gurudev Sadhu Vaswani. But I am helpless. I am not in my senses, I am not in control of my own life. It seems to me that I have hit the bottom of the pit. I am miserable. I am totally broken and unable to take on the trials and tribulations of life. My unhappy situation compels me to take this extreme step. Maybe, by the time you receive this letter, I will be no more. Forgive me, for I have decided to commit suicide."

You may rest assured that I took action on that sad letter: I called up some of our brothers and sisters, volunteers of the Mission from those parts. I requested them to lend all help and moral support to the lady and see to it that she did not do anything rash or hasty. But the letter made me think: why do people commit suicide? Why does a man or a woman reach a point where he or she is unable to carry on living? Why is it that the sufferings, challenges and disappointments of life, which billions upon billions of people face everyday, suddenly become impossible for these people to face? Why do they not think of any other alternative, but to end their life?

Throughout history, philosophers and psychologists have come to the conclusion that a pessimistic attitude, although justified in some circumstances, must be avoided, if man is to survive in an increasingly difficult environment. The study of pessimism is closely associated too, with the study of psychological depression. Aaron Beck, a psychiatrist, argues that depression is caused largely due to unrealistic negative views about human life and the world.

The number of suicides has been on the increase recently. All over the world the young and the old try to end their life. A disappointment in business, a failure in the examination, a loss on the stock exchange, a setback in a relationship, and even the common frustration of day-to-day living depresses them to such an extent, that they decide to put an end to their life. Even the youth, who are supposed to be optimistic, succumb to this extreme negativity. There are many who may not actually attempt suicide, but dwell constantly with the idea of ending their life when faced with a trying situation. Why do we succumb to this despair? Why do we entertain the idea of throwing away the invaluable gift of life?

The reason is pessimism. It is lack of faith in God. Man despairs when he thinks of his life in terms of failure and success. He despairs when he feels rejected or alienated. He succumbs to pessimism. He finds no purpose to his life.

But a man who is optimistic, who views the difficulties of life as challenges, will never think of committing suicide.

One of the important teachings of the *satsang* is that there is a meaning of mercy in whatever happens to us. We have taken this birth to imbibe the various lessons of life. Life is a school where we learn important lessons. Life is an arena of varied experiences. Each experience comes to us to teach us something.

An optimist has utter faith in God. "Whatever is happening is for my good. Whatever hurdles are there and whatever difficulties I have to face, they are to benefit me in terms of self growth and spiritual evolution." Once man realises this truth, he will never think of ending his life.

Let us be assured that whatever happens is for our benefit. This lesson should be taught to the students in schools and colleges. This lesson which brings the realisation of the inner value of all experience, gives man courage to cope up with every situation.

When I was in school, our teacher emphasised the importance of improving our handwriting. He often asked us to write out phrases and sentences. One of them was, "Every cloud has a silver lining". The dark nimbus clouds also have a silver lining somewhere because behind the clouds the sun shines and its rays light up the edges of dark clouds. For the time being the shining sun is covered by the clouds and once these clouds move out, the sun will shine brightly, spreading its splendour and warmth all around.

The great epic *Mahabharata* gives us the story of a *rishi*, who was extremely poor. He had no means to earn his living. Whatever he tried was a total failure. Somehow he managed to collect a small amount of money. He thought to himself that he would prosper, if only he could buy two bullocks with this money. He went to the market place and bought the bullocks, and took them back to his village, yoked together. As luck would have it, on his way back, a wild camel on a rampage, suddenly appeared on the scene and lifted the yoke so high that it strangulated both the animals. Both the bullocks fell dead on the ground. The *rishi*, who had entertained dreams about ploughing his fields with the help of oxen and reaping a rich harvest, was suddenly shattered. But this disheartening experience was the turning point in his life; for soon thereafter, he comes in contact with a holy man. The holy man conveys to him the following teaching: "Whenever you are faced with difficulties, whenever you experience frustration, whenever you suffer from an illness, whenever you are faced with hurdles, remember this one thing, that there is some deep, inner meaning in it. It is for your benefit." The *rishi* imbibes this teaching and becomes a realised soul.

We have a choice in life — the choice between optimism and pessimism. We can be either optimistic or pessimistic. A true optimist is indefatigable in his hopes. He will find a ray of hope; a hint of solution in every difficult situation. The optimist is fortunate because his outlook on life will always be positive and hopeful.

Have you heard those beautiful lines which I love to repeat:

> Two men stood behind prison bars;
> One saw mud, the other stars.

You can easily picture to yourself the situation described in these lines: there are two prisoners, locked up in a dark isolated cell in prison. For days together they stay in their dingy cells, unable to see the sunshine. One day, they are told, that they would be taken to the main gate of the prison. The gate would be closed but they would be able to see the outside world through the iron bars of the door. Both the prisoners go to the main gate. One looks up at the sky, gazes at the moon and its silvery beams, and the innumerable jewel-like stars which seem to be embedded in the dark blue velvet of the night sky. He is overwhelmed by the beauty of the vision he sees. He begins to hum a tune. As for the other prisoner, he looks down at the ground, and sees only dirt and filth. He says, "It is so dirty outside."

The first prisoner was an optimist. His companion was a pessimist!

There is a common puzzle or a conundrum, which is used to illustrate these two attitudes: does one regard a given glass of water, filled to half its capacity, as half *full* or as half *empty*? It is believed that optimists would reply, "Half full", and pessimists would respond, "Half empty" (assuming that "full" is considered good, and "empty", bad). When I was in school, I was given a picture of two buckets. Both the buckets were half-filled with water. One glass carried a smiling face with the words, "Thank God, I am atleast half full." And on the other there was a frowning face with the words, "Of what use is it to be half empty all the time?"

The concept of optimism is often linked with the name of Gottfried Wilhelm Leibniz, who held that we live in the best of all possible worlds, for he believed that God created a physical universe that follows the laws of physics, and was therefore perfect.

Personal optimism is said to be correlated to a healthy sense of self-esteem, which includes psychological well-being and physical and mental health. A distinguished academician, Martin Seligman, in researching this area, criticises psychologists for focusing too much on causes for pessimism and not enough on optimism. He says that he found through his research that in the last three decades of the 20th century, medical journals published 46,000 psychological papers related to depression and only 400 on inner peace and joy. In other words, even medical experts are obsessed with pessimism! Optimism, on the other hand, has been shown to be correlated with better immune systems in healthy people who have been subjected to stress.

In life we face many difficulties. We go through trying circumstances and heartbreaking situations. But we can face any difficulty, any challenge, if we are endowed with the optimistic bent of mind. Much depends on our perception and our reaction to a particular situation.

As for our perception, it has more bearing on our reactions than the reality that is around us. A man maybe passing through a dark night, but the dark night by itself may have no significance. Much depends on how he perceives the darkness and his attitude towards it. He may grow nervous, develop cold sweat, and suffer palpitations. Or he may breathe in the fresh, invigorating night air, and quietly hum a tune in solitude, as he walks along. It is all a matter of perception!

In the Srimad Bhagavad Gita, Lord Sri Krishna says, "O Arjuna, man is his own friend and his own foe." We are our own best friends and we are our own worst enemies. It is easy to put the blame on others for the difficulties that we encounter. A confirmed optimist puts it this way : "A pessimist sees only the dark side of the clouds, and mopes; a philosopher sees both sides, and shrugs; an optimist doesn't see the clouds at all – he's walking on them."

No man, no situation or circumstance can harm us if we have a positive attitude. For, a positive attitude is self-friendly and hence, it will never let you down. As Harry Truman once said, "A pessimist is one who makes difficulties of his opportunities and an optimist is one who makes opportunities of his difficulties."

It is true that life has a negative side, there is no denying this fact. Life is full of problems and difficulties, but we can cross all hurdles, solve all our problems and walk through all difficulties, if we have a positive attitude towards life. Therefore, optimism has been described as a kind of heart stimulant – the digitalis of failure!

Triumph belongs to thought. Change your thinking and you change your life! You become new!

As You Think, So You Become!

Today, scientists are beginning to understand the value and power of what is called 'thought energy'. They are beginning to study what our ancient *rishis* knew thousands of years ago. They taught their students *(Jignasus)* that a fundamental law of life is : "You become as you think."

I am indeed happy that this truth has been reaffirmed in our days by influential thinkers and scientists. One of the fundamental laws of life is that, 'Energy follows thought'. As we think, so we become. If we fear a fall, there is a possibility that we shall truly fall. To put it simply, we become what we think. Hence we should be very careful with our thoughts.

Thoughts have an inherent capacity to materialise.

Life gives us a choice between positivism and negativism. If you want to be a winner in life, then choose to be positive. A positive person is happy under all circumstances. His life has a 'subtle' energy which keeps him happy and contended.

It is not that the man with a positive attitude refuses to recognise that life has a negative side. He knows that life does have a negative side, a dark side. But the man of positive thinking refuses to dwell on the negative side. He looks for the best results from the worst conditions. And it is an inviolable law of life, that when you expect good, good will come to you!

Management experts narrate the following story to illustrate the benefits of positive attitude.

One day a farmer's donkey fell into a well. At first, the farmer was frantic; he wondered what he could do to rescue the stricken animal, which was crying out piteously from the depths of the disused well. With no obvious solution in sight, he came to the sad conclusion that as the donkey was old, and as the well needed to be filled in anyway, he should give up the idea of rescuing the beast, and simply fill in the well. Hopefully the poor animal would not suffer too much, he consoled himself.

The farmer asked for help from his neighbours. Soon, there were a dozen men briskly shovelling earth into the well. When the donkey realised what was happening, he wailed and struggled, but then, to everyone's relief, the wailing stopped after some time.

After a while the farmer looked down into the well and was astonished by what he saw. Not only was the donkey still alive, but he was progressing rapidly towards the top of the well. The so-called 'dumb' animal had discovered that by shaking off the earth instead of letting it cover him, he could keep stepping on top of the earth as the level rose. Soon the donkey was able to step up over the edge of the well, and he happily trot off.

Life tends to shovel dirt on top of each of us from time to time. The trick is to shake it off and take a step up.

How can you become positive? May I suggest that you follow a few simple rules:

1) Cultivate the spirit of acceptance – not just passive acceptance, but acceptance with faith and hope. Do your very best to achieve the result that you have in view. But inspite of your best efforts you are unable to succeed in your plans, you must learn to accept it as the will of God and say to yourself: "There must be a meaning to it." Get into the habit of accepting every situation, every circumstance as the Will of God. Acceptance with due gratitude is also a subtle law, which puts you on the path of self-growth. Accept all that happens to you with a simple prayer, "O God, whatever You do and whatever happens has a purpose and a meaning. Your scheme of things is perfect. I accept Your Will." This should be your attitude in life; and whether you succeed or fail, ever remain grateful to God!

Gurudev Sadhu Vaswani in his sacred verses says,
>Thank You, Thank You, O Lord,
>Grateful to You,
>Wherever I am.
>Whatever I am.
>*Shukkur.* I accept it all.

2) Whenever you face obstacles on your path, or problems that daunt you and seem to be beyond your control, seek God's help. To cross the hurdles, to solve the problems and to meet the challenges of life, you need inner strength, above all else. You can get this strength by appealing to the Supreme *Shakti*, the All-Powerful, the Almighty. Seek His strength. Appeal to Him: O Supreme *Shakti*, give me strength.

3) Train the mind. The mind, as our scriptures tell us, often behaves like a drunken monkey or like a wild horse. It has to be controlled; it has to be trained to shun negativism. Negative thoughts are a habit of the mind. Dispel negative thoughts and invite positive thoughts instead. You will find a change for the better in your life. Be firm with your mind. Resolve, here and now, that you will put up a 'No Entry' board to negativism. Block the rush of negative thoughts. Resolve, too, that you will put up the 'Welcome' sign and greet all positive thoughts. Convert your negative thoughts into positive ones. Replace the negative with the positive. You will experience calm and soothing vibrations not only within but also in your surroundings.

4) Believe that, 'This too shall pass away'. Tell yourself. "This trying time is here to test my faith. This stressful period will get over soon." For at the end of every tunnel is light, at the end of a dark night there is the beautiful dawn. The clouds spreading darkness hide the bright shining sun. Once the clouds pass away, the

sun will be visible, shining ever bright, spreading its warm radiance and light!

5) Keep your mind fully occupied. This will not only keep you away from worry and other wasteful thoughts, but will make the mind strong and constructive. Above all, learn to use your energy in the service of others. Pray for people who face greater difficulties than you do – for God knows that there are many of them. This will uplift your mind. Be an instrument of God and plough His field. Engage your mind in *satsang*. Read inspirational literature. As it is said:

> Lives of great men all remind us
> We can make our lives sublime…

6) Always remember, that God is with you. Tell yourself constantly: He is my Father and Mother. He is the One who protects all of us at all times. You have to have a direct hotline with God! You should talk to Him; have a dialogue with Him and sure enough He will show you the way. Build up faith in Him. Believe in Him.

If all else fails you, remember the Lord's promise to us in the Gita: *Renouncing all rites and writ duties, come to Me for single refuge* – seek refuge at His Holy Feet. He will never ever let you down!

Positive thinking is not instantaneous. To be positive, you have to put in effort. I am often told by a few friends, that in spite of much effort, some of them are unable to get rid of negativism. Maybe in some rare cases, one life is not sufficient to take away the negativism of numerous previous births. But you must continue your efforts ceaselessly, and some day out of the blue you will see, the clouds disperse and the sun shines brightly!

Man has been given free will. He has been given the right of choice. He can choose the path that leads to his betterment and well being and spiritual unfoldment. Or he can choose the path that leads to his degradation.

The Choice Is Yours!

It is perhaps true to say that in recent times, people are beginning to take their spiritual life seriously. They are devoting more time, attention and effort to spiritual matters. Many people also attend *satsang*. But how many of them know about the path to self-realisation? How many of them know the principles and ideals that they must follow in order to walk this path as genuine seekers? For I humbly submit, your physical presence at the *satsang* alone is not enough to ensure that you are a pilgrim on this path.

There are certain norms for those who wish to tread this spiritual path. There are certain ideals and principles of the life spiritual. One of the norms is beautifully described by Gurudev Sadhu Vaswani:

> Two cannot dwell in one heart,
> The World and God.
> O *jignasu*! Abandon your attachment
> To the world.
> Awake, Arise! Enshrine only One
> In your heart.

Make Him your Friend, Keep Him by your side,
O Nuri, Witness the Great Splendour,
Rejoice in the Beauty of the Beloved!
All the rest is dust, only dust!

This verse encapsulates a great lesson. There is place only for One in your heart. As the saying goes you cannot ride two horses, that of the World and that of God. Therefore, the Bible tells us: You cannot serve two masters – Mammon and God.

You have two options – be of the world, worldly; or be of the spirit, and turn your back upon worldly desires.

The choice is yours: either to enjoy the luxuries of the world or to make friends with the One who ever abides, who faileth not. You can go out into the world, and struggle hard for name, fame, position and status. Or you can sit in silence, and invite the Almighty to fill your heart with Divine Love.

You have to choose between the two paths – the easy, tempting, alluring worldly path which may give you power and wealth, but which will lead you to unhappiness and discontent; or the difficult, thorny and painful spiritual path, the path of yearning and intense aspiration, which will lead you to the Ultimate Bliss! For as sure as the sun rises in the East, it will lead you to the Realm of Light!

But first you have to make a choice. You have to decide for yourself, which path to follow, — and what goal you will try to achieve!

You will get what you really want! For this too is an inviolable Law of Nature. 'Ask and it shall be given unto you!' The Law of 'Ask and you shall be given' operates on certain principles. You have to ask, when the mind is integrated and focused. Normally, we ask for worldly things. We ask for all kinds of things, when the mind is turbulent. We ask continuously — we are not sure of what we really want from the Universe. The Universe is there to give us, to help us, and to reciprocate our thoughts and emotions! These secrets of the Universe are no longer hidden, but are open to all the people of the world.

Guru Nanak, in his sacred words says:

> Ask! Beg like a beggar.
>
> He, the Great Giver, will give, will surely give!
>
> He will surely comply with your request.

Hence, make a choice. Do not waste time. You have already lost precious time. You are lagging behind in achieving your goal. Wake up! Arise! Make up your mind. Decide now and here. Ask for what you want — and surely, it shall be given unto you!

If a child is asked, whether he would choose sugar-candy and chocolates or the melodious notes of Lord Krishna's Flute, obviously the child would choose sugar-candy and chocolates. Most of us are still children. We choose the glamour and sheen of the world. We hanker after worldly wealth. We fail to make the right choice. The right choice is of course, the melodious notes of Lord Krishna's flute, which is relayed from the Realm of Light!

One thing is for sure, you cannot divide your heart into two. You cannot partition it, and say, "Okay, one side I will reserve for the luxuries of the world, and on the other side, I will make room for the Almighty, the Illumined One." Jesus, more than two thousand years ago, had said the same thing, "You cannot serve two Masters at the same time!" Hence, choose your Master, for the choice is yours.

Sometime ago, I received a letter from a wealthy woman. She is the MD of a large company. She wrote that every morning, she made it a point to spend some time in silence. She tried to bond with the Invisible Infinite. She enjoyed communing with Him; she felt uplifted in His company. Afterwards, when she stepped into her corporate office, she was surrounded by worldly affairs. She had to take tough decisions to ensure that the company made profits. And there the conflict began – the conflict between Truth and Untruth. For earning profits these days, one has to juggle up figures and indulge in several 'acts of commission and omission'. The conflict became too much of a struggle for her. At times, she felt she was being torn apart, internally. In the letter, she asked for my advice as to what she should do.

How true it is, that you cannot ride two horses nor can you serve two Masters at the same time. If you attempt to do so, it may ultimately tear you apart.

This teaching, that you cannot have two masters at the same time, was given by Gurudev Sadhu Vaswani, to his spiritual daughter, Shanti. She was a radiant soul who joined the Beloved Master at the tender age of ten and continued to serve him loyally and devotedly till the end of His earthly pilgrimage.

Gurudev Sadhu Vaswani cautioned us against the allurements of this world. He said, "He who runs after worldly pleasures is no different from a thirsty man trying to quench his parched throat with the salt water of the ocean! Excessive salt water will only damage the intestines; it may even result in death." Our condition is no better. We try desperately to satisfy our desires but our desires keep on multiplying and there is no end in sight to extinguishing the ever-burning fires of *trishna*!

We will all do well to remember, that it is futile to run after material things. Even if we manage to accumulate wealth, we must bear in mind that it does not really belong to us. Can we take it along with us when we leave this earth? Will it 'buy' us accommodation in heaven? How pointless then, to think that our wealth belongs to us! We are merely trustees of worldly wealth that is placed in our hands. Everything belongs to Him, the Creator. The best use to which we can put our wealth is to spend it all judiciously, in the service of the poor and the broken ones.

Gurudev Sadhu Vaswani reminds us of this great truth. He urges us to break our bonds with the world of pleasures, and create space within the heart for Him alone. As the saying goes, "You cannot put two swords into one sheath". Similarly, you cannot give place to both 'World' and 'God' in your heart.

I am sure many young men and women will ask me, "When we live in the world, how can we ignore it? How can we turn our back upon life?" Yes. We live in the world, and we should have a zest for living. Life is God's greatest gift to us, and we should not be dead to this great gift. Treasure your life! Cherish this beautiful world and all of God's Creation! Therefore, love everyone. Love everything around you. Give the love of your beautiful heart to one and all. But do not be attached to the world. Love – Yes; attachment – No! Love without attachment – let this be the guiding star of your life. If you are attached to worldly things, your very attachment will sooner or later drag you into the dark pool of turbulence and passion.

Attachment and ego go together. Attachment puts a claim on people, wealth and status. 'I' and 'mine' become the properties of the 'ego'.

Gurudev Sadhu Vaswani, therefore, instructed Shanti, and through her all seekers on the path: "O, *jignasus*! Be not attached to the world. Awake! Arise! Cultivate friendship with the One and Only Fair!"

Every evening, Shanti would visit her family, and then, at night, she would return to the ashram, to be at the feet of her Master and Mentor, Sadhu Vaswani.

One day, Sadhu Vaswani said to her, "If you visit your family everyday, you may form an attachment to them. You have to decide, whether you want worldly attachments or friendship with God?" Shanti chose the path of 'detachment'. She chose friendship with God.

Often, when she fell ill, I would ask her, whether I should inform her sisters. She would smile and say, "No. Now I need no one. I have everything. I am at peace."

Attachments are distracting. They divert you from the goal that you must not lose sight of. These worldly attachments hound you when you sit in silence or in meditation. Thoughts of all the things to which you are attached begin to trouble you. And the still waters of silence become a whirlpool of stray thoughts. Detachment is necessary for meditation. Detachment is necessary for the trouble-free heart, the inner peace, the still point of calmness that we all yearn for.

Detachment is essential if you wish to tread the pilgrim path to self-realisation.

The spiritual path needs integration of thought, word and mind. It needs a focused mind that is free from desire and attachment. True, you cannot cut your bonds all of a sudden. You cannot detach yourself in an instant. It is a gradual process. It will take time. But you have to take the first step on the path and initiate the process of withdrawing from the world. It is better to do it today, rather than tomorrow; now, rather than later.

"Knowledge" makes a man proud. Love makes him humble. When knowledge is blended with love, man shines as do the angels of God. His life becomes radiant.

The Book Of The Heart Sufficeth!

There was a time when I was extremely fond of reading books. Let me confess, I had a passion for reading. Whenever the postman brought a parcel of books, I would be thrilled at the thought of all the pleasurable hours of reading that lay ahead. Nowadays, I hardly find time to read books. For, I have been taught, that it is better to meditate on the Name Divine than to read books.

Once, I happened to be in jail with Gurudev Sadhu Vaswani. Those were the days of India's freedom struggle. Gurudev Sadhu Vaswani was sentenced to be in prison for fourteen days, for leading a *satyagraha*. Sister Shanti, Gurudev Sadhu Vaswani's spiritual daughter, came to visit us, and to enquire whether there was anything in particular that we needed from home. I requested her to get me a trunk full of books. The very next day, Shanti brought me a whole load of books. Seeing this, the jailer was surprised. He said to me, somewhat sarcastically, "How long is your sentence – fourteen days or fourteen years? Why have you called for so many books? Will you actually manage to read all of them?"

As it happened, Gurudev Sadhu Vaswani's imprisonment caused an uproar across the whole town (Karachi). People began to agitate: they asked for a no-confidence motion to be passed against the cabinet. Within four days we were released and my trunk full of books was left in the prison. Gurudev Sadhu Vaswani said to me, "You are of the Eternal: the book of the heart sufficeth." On an earlier occasion, Gurudev Sadhu Vaswani had said to me. "You are fond of books. When will you start reading the book of all books, the only book that counts – the 'Book of your Heart'?"

After all, what do we get from reading books? We read a book, we ponder its contents, we hold discussions, and at the end of it all, what do we achieve? Therefore let me repeat Gurudev's words: read the Book of all books, the 'Book of your Heart'. Reading books may make a man a scholar, but it does not always give him wisdom or true knowledge. The 'Book of the Heart' is with everyone. You do not need to go to a library; it is there with you and within you. The 'Book of the Heart' is the 'Book of the Self'.

What is the Self? Is it the physical body or is it *that* which is beyond the physical – a part of that Infinite? The physical body is made of five elements. But You are not the body; the body is only a garment which you have worn in this life – a garment which you have changed innumerable times during the endless adventure of existence.

Our true self is not the gross physical; it is beyond birth and death. But because we have identified ourselves with the physical self, we commit the great blunder of celebrating our so-called birthdays. They are not our birthdays. They are the birthdays of the physical body.

The truth is, as the Gita tells us, we are not born, nor do we die. We are Immortal, Eternal, Immutable, Deathless; weapons cannot cleave us, fires cannot burn us, waters cannot drown us and the winds cannot dry us away. We are THAT! *Tat Twamasi!* Man's greatest illusion is his identification with the body. We are not born and we do not die. We realise this when we make a study of the 'Book of the Heart'.

Once we have crossed this illusion we realise that our true self is immortal. This realisation will relieve us of many other illusions, which we labour under constantly, here on this earth. These illusions arise in the first place, because we think we are this body of five elements and five senses. Identifying our 'self' with this body, we get upset at the slightest aberration; we despair at the slightest failure.

Once a woman came to me with tears in her eyes. She wept as she said to me, "My son has married a girl from another community. I feel quite, quite miserable." I said to her, "Why should you be ashamed of your son, if he has married a girl from another community? Marriage is a matter of *karma*, it is probably a result of the actions of our previous births. What makes you feel so miserable?"

Not long ago, a man came to meet me: at one time he had been a millionaire. But in, what they call a 'global melt down process' he had lost much of his wealth. He said to me, "I feel very small and defeated." I said to him, "Money will come and money will go. In an uncertain world, everything is uncertain. Why should you feel inferior to others, just because you have lost money? Why should your self-esteem depend upon your wealth? Your self-esteem should come from your inner strength. You are of the Eternal. Your Spirit is pure *Shakti*. You have nothing to fear of and nothing to lose. You have the abundant *shakti* within which has its source in the Infinite, the All-Powerful Almighty. You may have lost your money; but the infinite treasure of divine *shakti* is still within you."

You have to be aware of the *shakti* within and you will be able to achieve all that you desire.

The question arises, "What may we do to become aware of the *shakti* within?"

Scientists have tried to explore the vast realms of space. They have tried to conquer the forces of nature. We are talking of establishing colonies in space. We are harnessing wind and waves and sunlight to produce alternative supplies of energy. Yet, our knowledge of man's inner *shakti* is limited. We must now concentrate on the search for the *shakti* which is infinite. The meaning of the words 'search' is to explore deeply. Just as scientists explore nature we should explore the *shakti* within us.

"Know Thyself" is what the saints and sages have said to us repeatedly. The Ancient Greek aphorism "Know Thyself" was said to be inscribed in the forecourt of the famous Temple of Apollo at Delphi, according to ancient Greek philosophers. This obviously did not mean understanding one's habits and values and attitudes; it was always given a mystical interpretation. 'Thyself', is not meant in reference to the lower self which we call the ego, but the Higher Self above and beyond the ego – the I AM consciousness. As for India's ancient sages, they went one step beyond 'Know Thyself'. They asserted emphatically; *That art Thou! Tat twamasi!*

Tat Twam Asi is one of the *Mahâvâkyas* (Grand Pronouncements) in Vedantic Hinduism. It originally occurs in the *Chandogya Upanishad*. In other words that Brahman which is the common reality behind everything in the cosmos, is the same as the essential Divinity, namely the *Atman* within you. It is this identity which is the grand finale of *Upanishadic* teaching, according to the *Advaita* philosophy of Adi Shankara. *Tat twamasi!* This awareness can only come to us through intuitive experience, meditation, deep introspection and, above all, through the grace of God and the Guru. It is totally different from any objective experience. It cannot be inferred from books or discourses or other forms of learning and reading. Therefore Gurudev Sadhu Vaswani urged us, "Read the book of your heart!" For this alone can lead to true Self-knowledge.

"Know Thyself" is a fundamental tenet of those who wish to arrive at the true meaning of life, the purpose of this human existence. If we really wish to know our true self, this will involve us in a deeply personal, spiritual transformation, an experience that will reveal the essence of the spirit within us.

But to find the 'self' is not easy; one has to go deep within and search for it. For this we need someone to guide us on the journey and show us the path. It is only the Guru, who can guide us on this journey and give us the necessary directions we need on the road to self-discovery. Any individual would find it difficult to take this journey alone. *"Kaun Batave Vaat Guru Bin?"* In other words, *who will indicate to us the Way, except the Guru?* The Guru will tell us, how to go within. He will reveal to us how to go within and open the 'Book of the Heart' and under His grace and guidance, we will discover the great truth – I am *That*.

We should have the yearning to seek a true Guru. It is said that one need not go in search of a Guru. The Guru himself will come in search of his disciples; provided the disciple is ready to undertake the spiritual journey. This is one of the rules of spiritual life – When the disciple is ready the Guru appears.

Sri Ramana Maharshi was one of those great souls who constantly urged his followers to seek the true self within. Whenever people asked him to teach them the way to Liberation, he recommended self-enquiry as the fastest path to *moksha*. His primary teachings are documented in a book which is very significantly titled, *Naan Yaar?* (Who am I?). Here he tells us: all living beings desire to be happy, for happiness is our true nature. But to attain to that happiness, one should know one's true Self. For that, the path of knowledge, the *gyaana maarga*, the inquiry "Who am I?", is the principal means.

Here are a few of his precepts:

- Of all the thoughts that rise in the mind, the thought 'I' is the first thought.
- The mind will subside only by means of the enquiry 'Who am I?' The thought 'Who am I?', destroying all other thoughts, will itself finally be destroyed like the stick used for stirring the funeral pyre.
- If one then enquires 'Who am I?' the mind (power of attention) will turn back to its source. By repeatedly practising thus, the power of the mind to abide in its source increases.
- The place where even the slightest trace of the 'I' does not exist, alone is Self.
- Self itself is the world; Self itself is 'I'; Self itself is God; all is the Supreme Self *(Siva Swarupam)*.

However, Sri Ramana Maharishi cautioned us against considering self-enquiry as an empty, abstract, intellectual exercise. This is why, although his primary teaching was self-enquiry, he advised the practice of self-surrender (to one's Deity or Guru) as an alternative means, which would ultimately converge on to the path of Self-Enquiry. You must wipe out the ego, in order to read the Book of the Heart. You must conquer the ego self, to arrive at the true knowledge of the Self.

Jalal-u-din Rumi was one of the greatest scholars the world has known. He wrote many books, he read many scriptures. His students lived in awe of him. One day, Rumi heard a knock on his door. He opened the door and found a man standing there. His name was Shams-e-Tabriz. Both gazed at each other. Rumi was wonderstruck. He thought, "Who could this man be"? Then the Light of recognition shone in his eyes. At once, Rumi fell at the feet of this man. Rumi could recognise the Guru in him. Shams-e-Tabriz picked up Rumi's manuscripts and threw them in a river. Rumi was shocked. His hard-work of many years was destroyed within a minute. He began to weep. He said, "I loved my books more than my children." Shams-e-Tabriz, seeing the plight of his disciple, consoled him with the words, "Read the 'Book of your Heart'. For you are of the Eternal."

This marked the beginning of Rumi's spiritual journey. He went deep within and wrote beautiful poetry, timeless poetry. Centuries have passed, yet Rumi's poetry is read with great fervour and devotion even now. His book *Masnavi* is a marvellous work. I too, read it sometimes. This book is a rare treasure.

We have received this birth to know our true self. We should explore and study the 'Book of our Heart'. For when we go to the other shore we will leave behind everything, except the knowledge of the Self which is an emanation of the Supreme Self, that for want of a better word we call God. *Tat twamasi*, That art Thou! It is this knowledge alone that has any real value.

Peace will never come from external things. It comes when you are anchored in the changeless, settled in the God within.

The Easiest Way To Peace

Recently, an earnest young man came to meet me. He said to me in all sincerity, that he had listened to my discourses on the Gita, and practical suggestions on the three *margas* (ways) indicated in the Gita by Sri Krishna – namely, the Paths of *Gnana, Karma* and *Bhakti*. He referred to Sri Krishna's promise: "On whatever path men approach me, on that I go to meet them! For all the paths are mine, verily mine!" He had a problem: he felt overwhelmed by the rigours of the threefold paths; he felt that he simply could not 'measure up' to any one of them. "Surely, Dada," he pleaded, "there must be an easier way open for novices, people like me, who aspire to God, but hesitate to take the first step forward?"

I assured him that there was, indeed, an easier way forward; perhaps the quickest and shortest route for a seeker.

Let me tell you about the sacred words of *Sri Sukhmani Sahib*:

Anek Jivan Janamiye Maar Jaa-m,
Naam Japat Pave Bisram!

Guru Arjan Dev tells us: In this endless adventure of existence you have wandered through many births. If only you will meditate on the Name divine, you will find rest.

Sant Kabir gives us the same teaching in unforgettable terms:

Hat-a hat-a bikai

In the endless cycle of birth and death you have been sold from market to market.

How can we attain freedom from this endless cycle of birth and death? Man wants peace, man wants bliss, but he is caught in this cycle of birth and death which he cannot break.

Guru Nanak has shown us an easy path, a path that leads to peace and bliss. It is the path of the Name Divine. Man has gone through many experiences of joy and sorrow. His life bears scars of many tragedies. He has shed tears of sorrow which could fill oceans.

Once, Gautama Buddha sat under a tree: around him were the *bhikkhus*. The Buddha said to them, "The word bhikkhu means a beggar." So many of the Buddha's disciples were from royal families. They were brought up in the lap of luxury. They gave up their all to sit at his holy feet. They gave up the comforts of life and joined the Buddha, taking refuge in the words of the mantra:

Buddham Sharanam Gachchami
Dhamam Sharanam Gachchami
Sangham Sharanam Gachchami.

And the Buddha said to them, "Great has been your suffering through innumerable births. You have wept tears of sorrow, tears which, if collected, would surpass the waters of the four oceans."

Guru Arjan Dev in his sacred lyrics tells us:

Sagal Srisht Ka Raja Dukhiya
Har Ka Naam Japat Hoi sukhiya.

Everyone in this world is unhappy. Even the sovereign of the entire world is unhappy. Happy, indeed, is the man who sings the Name Divine.

If you want to be at peace within, if you wish to be truly happy, but do not know how to go about it, like the young man who came to me, then follow the *Sahaj marg*, the easy path, the path of the Name Divine. This path is open to all. It is available to everyone. It is the path of reciting the Name Divine. No amount of material wealth can bring you the happiness you seek. No amount of worldly pleasures can bring this happiness; for, as Gurudev Sadhu Vaswani says, even the King, with all his power and wealth, is unhappy.

You may have heard of an American millionaire, who had everything a man could desire, including wealth, name, fame, and all the pleasures of life that money could buy. Yet he was found dead on the ground, a pistol by the side of the dead body. This wealthy millionaire – Barton by name, had committed suicide. In a note which he had left behind, he had written, "I feel miserable, I do not wish to live anymore."

I often mention this incident to my friends, so that they are not misled by the thought that riches and fame will make them happy, contented and fulfilled. I urge them that they would be better off, chanting the Name Divine, instead of craving after riches.

Let me assure you by chanting the Name Divine, you will find true bliss.

What do I mean by the Name Divine? Our sages and saints constantly speak to us of the 'Name Divine'. According to them there is a Supreme *Shakti* that governs this universe from end to end. By this Supreme *Shakti*, is the universe sustained and supported. By this Supreme *Shakti* all the worlds in all the Universes are controlled.

The *Shakti* is within us. The man who is aware of it is, verily, an awakened man.

How may this *Shakti*, that is within us be awakened? So, let me tell you a story about Guru Nanak. Guru Nanak sat in meditation on Mount Sumeru, when three *Yogis* belonging to Gorakhnath Panth met him and asked Him a number of questions to which Guru Nanak gave appropriate answers. These questions and answers are quoted in the *Japji Sahib*.

The *Yogis* asked Guru Nanak to describe the Realm of Light and tell them how they could have a glimpse of that Realm which Guru Nanak called *Sach Khand*? Guru Nanak said, to have a glimpse of that realm we must meditate, chant the Name Divine. The psyche of him who wakes up at the beautiful hour of *Amrit Vela* to meditate, experiences the purity of the vibrations of that hour.

He gets beautiful visions of the other worlds. He receives messages from beyond for the benefit of mankind. He gets in tune with the Infinite Energy of the Name Divine.

It is sad that the 'lifestyle' of so many of us now, is not conducive to this kind of practice. Many young men and women keep late hours, either working or pleasure-hunting and go to sleep at this sacred hour of 4 a.m. in the morning! They miss out on the pure vibrations of that hour. They live purely on the physical level and therefore their emotions are often base and troublesome.

You must bow down to the Guru and ask for strength to wake up at that early hour. Wake up at 3 o'clock: and if you cannot manage it, try to wake up at 4 o'clock; if you still cannot, try 5 o'clock. Avail of this holy hour even if it is for a short time. Chant the Name Divine and experience beautiful vibrations. I assure you, if you do this just once or twice, you will wish to do it again and again: you will form a good habit. But remember, I said, wake up at 4 a.m.

or 5 a.m. to meditate and chant the Name Divine – not to attend to your routine chores or your office work!

If you so much as take a dip in the Ganga of devotion at this sacred hour, you will experience the peace that passeth, surpasseth understanding!

Happiness does not come from material things. True happiness comes from within. True happiness is a child of inner peace.

For many of us today, *tyaga and tapasya, dhyan and yagna,* are difficult *sadhanas*. So the Gurus have indicated an easy way – the way of repeating the Name Divine. Therefore, start right away: chant the Name Divine in the ambrosial hours of the dawn. Sing His glories. Realise His greatness. Catch a glimpse of that Supreme *Shakti* in the lives of saints and sages – the holy ones who have borne witness to the Truth.

When you chant the Name Divine, your heart and mind are transformed. You get an insight into the meaning and purpose of human birth. And you will grow in the milk of human kindness, which will inspire you to reach out to those in need, to offer a helping hand to those who are weary and heavy-laden on the rough road of life.

There are many noble instances in the history of mankind inspiring us to serve others with humility and reverence. Abraham Lincoln, the President of America, was a great man. One day he saw a small child carrying a heavy load. The child was panting and out of breath. Abraham Lincoln went up to the child and said, "May I help you, my child! Let me carry this heavy trunk for you." Just imagine, a President of a country carrying a trunk on his back to help a child! True greatness lies in humility and kindness. Abraham Lincoln was truly a great man. Nobility of the heart comes from love within. Where there is love, there is kindness and there is humility.

One day, Gurudev Sadhu Vaswani was on his daily walk when he noticed an old woman carrying a heavy load on her back. The bag was so heavy that the old woman was bent beneath the load. Gurudev did not ask any of his disciples to help the old woman. Instead, he himself walked up to the old woman and said, "Let me carry your load." The old woman did not know who it was who volunteered to carry her heavy load. She gladly gave the bag to Sadhu Vaswani. Gurudev carried the load on his back with a smile, and accompanied the woman to her cottage. He then took out a silver coin and giving it to the old woman said to her: "Mother, bless me." This is true nobility of the heart. The great ones are also the humble ones.

We too, must resolve to serve someone every day. Wipe the tear of a poor one, feed the hungry, give water to the thirsty, give grains to birds. We must see that we do at least one act of service every day. At night before going to sleep let us ask ourselves, if we have done any good deed that day. We need to bear witness to the teachings of our great Gurus in deeds of daily living.

Firstly, we need to study and reflect on the teachings of our Gurus and the great ones. The emphasis in their teaching is on love. Love God and love thy neighbour as thy self. Secondly, we must make an effort to express our love in action. We must be gentle and kind and be of service to others. If we do so, we will in due course be blessed with peace that passeth, surpasseth understanding. It may not be long before we are released from the cycle of birth and death.

To meditate on or to chant the Holy Name of God, we need to withdraw our senses from the outer world. The mind, led by the senses, wanders in all the ten directions. It must be focussed on the Name Divine. Close your eyes to the outside world, shut your ears to the outside noise, and hear the Inner Symphony. *"Sunta Nahi Dhun Ki Khabar, Anahad Ka Baja Bajeta."* Within you sounds the unstruck music: alas, you hear it not! For, your ears are eager to listen to noises of the outside world.

Control the five senses and you will be filled with indescribable peace.

Enter the chamber of the heart and behold the Beauteous One seated on its throne. Before you can do this, you have to close the nine gates of the human body that distract you, day and night. When the nine gates are closed, the tenth hidden door opens and you can behold the wonders of the wonderful One. The journey begins by chanting, in fellowship with the devotees of the Lord, the Name Divine. Chant the Name Divine, O ye whose hearts long for a vision of the Beloved! Sing the Holy Name and bear witness in deeds of daily living, to the teaching of saints and sages. Such is the way to Peace!

Say NO to negative emotions like jealousy, envy, anger and resentment : fill your mind with vibrations of joy, peace, love and harmony.

Learn To Say, 'No'!

At a question-answer session, I was asked: "You often speak of the purpose of life. Can you tell us what that purpose is?" My answer was: "The purpose of life is to grow in perfection, from more to more. I must not seek to be more perfect than others, but I should try to see that I am more perfect today than I was yesterday and that tomorrow I will be more perfect than I am today." Jesus said: "Be ye perfect as your Father in Heaven is perfect."

The goal that every one of us must place before ourselves is to be a perfect human being. It was George Fisher who said: "When you aim for perfection, you discover it's a moving target." In other words, it is not easy to be a perfect man. It is a long difficult journey, on which one has to surmount many obstacles and cross many hurdles. This difficulty is compounded by the fact that as man is, he, is restless. Man, by temperament, tends to wander aimlessly, pushed by desires and fuelled by ambition. Nevertheless, the pursuit of perfection is a worthy goal; and all of us must strive for it.

The Perfect Man too, has wandered much. He has wandered long. He has wandered far and wide. But a stage comes in his life when he finds his anchor, and defines his goal. The average man is a prisoner of desires. Desires push him here and there. He spends his whole life wandering in the wilderness of worldly illusions and desires! And, as we all know, desires have a way of multiplying. Our saints and sages have warned us that desires are like fire, and foolish as we are, we try to quench them by satisfying them. This is as bad as trying to put out fire, by pouring *ghee* on to it! The more *ghee* we pour, the more we fan the flames and the more uncontrollable grows the fire.

To quench the fire of desires, we do not need *ghee*. We need the pure waters of the Spirit.
Guru Arjan Dev, in his sacred words says:
> The Perfect Man does not lose his balance.
> The Perfect Man has tasted the joys of desirelessness.

This, then, is the first mark of a man of perfection. He is without desires. He has learnt to say No – not to others, but to himself.

The trouble with most of us is that we have not learnt to say No to ourselves. The satisfied man, the perfect man has learnt to say No. We yield to greed. We yield to temptation. The perfect man has learnt to say NO to the greed for gold, to the temptations of sense-gratification. He has learnt to say No, when people come to honour him, to shower him with praise and to flatter him. He does not need such praise to boost his ego, or indeed to know his own self-worth. He has seen through the veil of *maya*.

There was a man who attended *satsang* every day. One day his conscience was stirred. He realised that he had been running after money and wealth throughout his adult life. He had millions in the bank account. He had successfully evaded Income tax by manipulating his accounts. His conscience now made him aware of his many sins of commission and omission; he realised that he had amassed enough money and there was no need to run after more. Inspired and moved by the soul-stirring discourse he had heard at the *satsang* that day, he made a firm resolve that he would now get over his greed for more and more money, and focus instead on the call of the spirit.

The following day, he received a call from his friend who lived abroad, telling him that new equity shares were on the stock market and that it would be a golden opportunity of investment. He was assured that his money would double in a very short time. Only a few hours earlier, he had resolved that he would stop hankering after money; but when he received the call, he forgot all about his good resolution and immediately made arrangements for some of his unaccounted money to be sent through illegal means to his friend abroad, to be invested in the new shares floated in the stock market. This man was not fixed on his goal. He had not learnt to say NO. He did not have the strength of will to tell his friend that he was not interested in any new investment. He was quite carried away by his friend's tempting offer.

The Perfect Man has learnt to say NO. That is the best way to get rid of desires. Every one of us has some weakness or the other. Many of us have a weakness for good food. Some of us have a weakness for affluence and status. We often succumb to our weaknesses because we have not learnt to say NO.

At the Sadhu Vaswani Mission, we collect pledges every year from people who promise to go without food of violence (non-vegetarian food), during the birthday celebrations of our beloved Gurudev Sadhu Vaswani, who, as you all know, was a messiah of Compassion, and a Prophet of reverence for all Life. I know of people who pledge to be vegetarians, but when a plate of *kababs* appears before them, they are tempted to eat it in spite of taking the pledge! Who are we to judge them? They must be answerable to their own conscience. Such men and women lack the courage to say NO. Faced with a platter full of the food they have abjured, they do not have the inner strength to say, "Take it away from here, I will not eat it. I have pledged to stay away from this food."

Learning to say No, is the first step towards perfection. It can take you forward in your spiritual life.

Each one of us must strive to become a perfect human being. Do not wait for tomorrow. Make the beginning *today*, *now*, so you can move closer to liberation in this birth. The more you give in to your desires, the more you wander, the longer it will take for you to make that crucial U-turn and get back to the source. Be firm in your resolution. Learn to say NO.

Andrew Carnegie, a famous industrialist, was born in Scotland and immigrated to the US. He began his career by doing odd jobs and with luck and hard work he became one of the wealthiest men in America. He was a steel magnate. Andrew Carnegie earned millions of dollars. One day he asked himself, "What will I do with so much money?" When he had no answers to this question, he adopted a guideline for himself – that he would take for his own use only as much money as was required to give him and those that depended on him – his family members and others - a comfortable living. All the profits earned over and above that, would go into charity. He put a limit to his expenses. Subsequently, with all the extra money that he earned, he started the Andrew Carnegie Foundation. The foundation was created to open schools, colleges, hospitals, museums and research laboratories. The foundation generated employment, it contributed to social upgradation of the people in the community. It helped in the development of villages. All this was possible because of just one man, who learnt to say NO. His famous words are still remembered by many American philanthropists: "When you die rich, you die disgraced".

How I wish that more of us could imbibe this lesson and donate at least some of the extra money we earn for good causes! We should donate money in charity without expecting anything in return – not even a word of thanks. Selfless service is also an instrument of spiritual growth and self evolution. Through service of mankind we can wipe away our bad karmas.

We save money for the future of our children. We save money for the security of our own old age and retirement. But there should be a limit to this. How much can you leave for your children? Too much money and too much luxury will only spoil them! Let your children learn the value of hard work and become self dependent. Let them learn the value of money. Take care of them, provide security for them, but at the same time spend some money in the service of others.

Jafar Saddique was a *dervish,* who was a trader by profession, but he was detached from money. One day, due to strange and unforeseen circumstances, people accused Jafar of having stolen a bag of money. It was indeed unfortunate that a *dervish* and a true *fakir* like him should become the object of people's blame. Jafar asked his accusers, "Tell me, what did the stolen bag contain?" People replied, "The bag contained a thousand *dinars.*" On hearing this Jafar went to his house and picked up a bag; he put thousand *dinars* in it. Handing it over to the people he said, "Take your thousand *dinars.*" The people started whispering, "So, our suspicion was right. This man has returned the money that he had stolen."

After two months, the thief who had stolen the bag was caught. He confessed that it was he who had stolen the thousand *dinars*. People felt ashamed of themselves and said, "We have degraded this man of God. This man was innocent, but we put the blame on him. Without uttering even a word of protest, he gave away thousand *dinars*." Then the people took the *dinars* and went to return the amount to the *dervish*. They said to him, "O *dervish*, forgive us and take back your thousand *dinars*." Jafar Saddique replied, "I do not take back what I give."

Just imagine, the *dervish* does not take back the money which rightfully belonged to him. Such men have learnt to say NO to greed of money. Learn to say No to temptation, whether it be the temptation of money, temptation of reward, name, fame or status.

You should learn to say No to flattery and sycophancy. You may appreciate others, but if any one flatters you, fold your hands and refuse to acknowledge it.

St. Anthony lived on a mountain top. Sometimes he went into the nearby towns. He was a great man with tremendous charisma. Wherever he went, people followed him. People heard his words with attention and imbibed his teachings eagerly. One day, he went to a town. After staying there for a few days he decided to go back. When people came to know of it, they felt sad. There were tears in the eyes of men, women and children. They wept, "How can you leave us? Please do not go, for we need you here amongst us."

The people went to the King and said to him, "St. Anthony is leaving us, kindly plead with him to stay back in our town." The king agreed and went to meet St. Anthony, inviting him to stay in the royal palace. The saint did not give any answer to the king; when people asked him about it, he avoided the whole issue by saying that he would consider the request later, may be the following day. In his mind St. Anthony thought, "If I have to run away, I might as well do so in the night. If I stay till the morning, then people will force me to stay here." And so, he actually left the town in the night. He knew his place was not in the hustle and bustle of the town. He had chosen to live a life apart from the crowds, apart from the pleasures and perils of the workaday world. To his austere life of solitude and simplicity, he chose to return, spurning the adulation of the people as well as the royal invitation.

Learn to say No. Do not succumb to your weaknesses. Be firm with yourself.

Once a *dervish* was asked, "Mahatma, how did you attain such spiritual heights?" He replied, "I followed one principle; whenever my mind said: 'answer back,' I would keep silent."

On the contrary, whenever we are asked a question, we are prompt to react. If the question is an unpleasant one or the remark is hurting, we are quick to give back word for word, abuse for abuse. We become worldly. We get entangled in squabbles and petty fights.

A brother once said to me, "The *satsang* I go to is really good. It is the best snack and juice bar I have ever come across."

Puzzled, I asked him "Why do you say so?"

He replied, "In our *satsang* we get different varieties of *prasad* everyday; sometimes it is *gulab jamun*, sometimes *samosa*, sometimes *pav bhaji*, sometimes *vada pav*, and sometimes ice cream. All the things which I love to eat, which are quite expensive outside, are available here for free."

I said to him, "I see your point. You get delicious snacks, so your *satsang* is like a snack bar. But why do you call it a juice bar?"

He thought for a while but could not reply. I said to him, "You are right, this *satsang* is truly a snack and a juice bar. You receive *prasad* of delicious savouries, and you get the juice (essence) of the Name Divine. In this *satsang*, you get both food for the stomach and food for the soul. Don't neglect one for the other."

Drink the nectar of the Name Divine
Slake your thirst with the waters of the spirit.

Once you taste this nectar, you would not like to be entangled with worldly affairs.

The Perfect man is one who has learnt to say No, to worldly temptations. He has tasted the nectar of the bliss divine.

God is the ultimate source of power in our life. Let us ensure that, the circuit between him and us is never broken. "Let us stay connected to God through the healing power of his Name."

A Simple And Easy Way To God

I think *bhakti* is one of the most beautiful, most powerful words that I have ever come across. Scholars and experts tell us that it was first given its full explication and significance in the Song of the Lord, the Bhagavad Gita. As we all know, Sri Krishna recommends the *bhakti marga* or the way of devotion, to his dear, devoted disciple Arjuna, as the easiest and simplest way to reach Him:

> Fix thy mind on Me; be devoted to Me; worship Me; bow down to Me. Thus having controlled thyself, and making Me thy Goal Supreme, thou shalt come unto Me.
>
> *Gita chapter IX-34*

We are told that *bhakti* is derived from the root word *bhaj* – which means 'to share', 'to belong', 'to participate'. I am sure we can recognise in this Sanskrit root, the origins of the word that is familiar to all of us, namely *bhajan*.

Bhakti is devotion. *Bhakti* is worship. *Bhakti* is participation and involvement in the act of worship.

Above all, *bhakti* is pure, unadulterated love for the Divine!

Sant Keshavdas, narrating the story of Shabari, tells us that this great woman saint sat at Sri Rama's feet and asked him, "Among all the spiritual disciplines, which pleases you the most? How can we attain to you most easily? I ask you this, on behalf of all your devotees." And Sri Rama said to her:

"Such pure devotion is expressed in nine ways... First is *satsang* or association with love-intoxicated devotees. The second is to develop a taste for hearing my nectar-like stories. The third is service to the guru... Fourth is to sing my *kirtan* ... *Japa* or repetition of my Holy name and chanting my *bhajans* are the fifth expression ... To follow scriptural injunctions always, to practise control of the senses, nobility of character and selfless service, these are expressions of the sixth mode of *bhakti*. Seeing me manifested everywhere in this world and worshipping my saints more than myself is the seventh mode of *bhakti*. To find no fault with anyone and to be contented with one's lot is the eighth mode of *bhakti*. Unreserved surrender with total faith in my strength is the ninth and highest stage. Shabari, anyone who practices even one of these nine modes of my *bhakti* pleases me most and reaches me without fail. That which is most difficult for the greatest *yogis* was easily attained by you, Shabari, because of your sincere devotion. This is the testimony of my *bhakti*."

I am told that in the UK and USA, there are groups of people whose mission it is to promote atheism. Various non-believers under an umbrella organisation called the British Humanist Association have decided to 'promote the cause of atheists' by buying advertising space on London Transport buses, and publicising slogans such as *There is probably no God* and *You can be good without God*, etc.

The Hindu faith is so liberal, broadminded and tolerant, that it has room even for atheists under its fold! The Charvaka school of philosophy, for example, is one such materialistic or atheist school, which denies the existence of the soul and of God! In fact, we have several religious traditions in India that reject and deny the scriptural authority of the *Vedas*, and effectively discourage worship of any deity. This includes Sikhism, Jainism, Buddhism, as well as the Charvaka materialists and others.

Once, a young man confronted Gurudev Sadhu Vaswani. He asked, "You talk so much about God. Tell me, who is God?" Sadhu Vaswani replied, "If you doubt the existence of God, it is clear that you know nothing about God. We say God is our protector, God is our caretaker, and God is kind and forgiving. All this is true. But, God is infinite. To define God is to deny Him, for He is beyond the mind and the senses, and you can never hope to grasp Him by your reason alone! He cannot be described in words. For that infinite power is beyond the perception of the human senses and intellect."

God is infinite; our intellect is finite; therefore we apprehend one or two aspects of the All Powerful One. We think of Him as our parent: *tu mata pita, ham balak tere...*; we think of Him as the all-knowing One: *Prabhu tum antaryami...* We think of Him as the personification of kindness and compassion: *Deena bhandu Deena naath...* He is *Data, Vidaata,* He is the King of Kings... Of course all these assertions are true; but they represent only a fraction of the whole truth.

Surely you remember the story of the blind men who began to argue about the shape and the form and the size of the elephant. Like them we are only partially aware of what God really is. If we were really wise, we would say, "The elephant was so huge; but I touched only a very small part of it. How can I tell you about the whole?"

This human limitation, in trying to grasp the nature of God, is brought out beautifully in an incident from the life of St. Augustine. It is said that he was engaged in a profound reflection on the nature of the Holy Trinity, and had spent several days and nights pondering over this concept and trying to put it all into words. One evening, he was walking on the beach, deep in thought, trying to unravel the mystery, when he saw a small boy using a seashell to carry water from the sea to pour into a hole he had made on the beach.

St. Augustine was amused by the sight. He asked the boy, "What do you think you are doing?"

"Can't you see?" the boy replied. "I have dug a hole there, and I am going to empty the ocean into it with the help of this sea shell."

The saint laughed. We laugh too, when we hear the story. But the boy had taught St. Augustine a valuable lesson: philosophers and theologians (and, in our own way, all of us) are really just as foolish, trying to do the same thing by attempting to define and describe God. We try to fathom the nature of the Divine, with help of the human intellect which is so finite, so inadequate for the purpose! Even as the eye cannot hear and the ear cannot see, even so the tiny human intellect cannot encompass the vastness of the Eternal God.

Let me give you the story of the salt doll, which is from an ancient Indian legend:

A salt doll journeyed for thousands of miles over the land, until it finally came to the sea. It was fascinated by this vast, moving mass of water, quite unlike anything it had ever seen.

"Who are you?" said the salt doll to the sea.

The sea replied with a smile, "Why don't you come in and see."

So the doll waded into the blue waters. As it walked farther and farther into the sea, it began to dissolve, until only a small, minute fraction of its form was all that was left. Before the last bit dissolved, the doll exclaimed in wonder, "Now I know who you are!"

This story tells us that the best way to 'know God' is to become like the salt doll. Even as the doll ceased to exist in the immensity of the ocean, so too, we must be prepared to lose our identity and become a drop in the vastness, the magnificence that is God. We must make the effort to become one with God.

When man goes beyond thoughts and words, when he goes beyond the mind, then he goes through many extraordinary experiences. He experiences bliss. Such bliss, *ananda*, is also a form of *bhakti*. We all can experience this bliss, if we make the effort; but we are so engrossed in the world of thoughts and words and physical activities, that such an experience is just lost to us, for want of trying!

It is said that King Louis VI of France had a friend who had been his classmate during boyhood. Later, as their ways parted, Louis became the sovereign, and the friend became a monk, and a devoted disciple of St. Francis. One day, King Louis remembered his boyhood friend. Out of respect for the monastic way of life, the King himself went to the monastery where he resided, rather than send for him to visit the palace. There was great excitement in the monastery as the King arrived. How would the King greet his friend? What would the monk say to the King?

The King and the monk were closeted together for over two hours. For two hours they sat with each other, without speaking a word to each other. In silence they sat and in silence they parted. After this meeting with his childhood friend, King Louis bowed down to him and took his leave. The other monks gathered around their colleague and asked him, "What did the king say to you? And what did you say to the king?" The King's friend replied, "Whatever we had to communicate to each other, we communicated in silence. The profoundest and greatest truths are communicated through silence."

Silence helps us to hear the inner voice. Everyday, we must learn to sit in silence for sometime, preferably early in the morning, so that we may begin the day with silence. By doing so, you will feel peaceful. God has no language, His only language is Love.

God is infinite, God is beyond description. Even the holy scriptures, the *Vedas* and *Upanishads* have not been able to give an adequate description of the Infinite Omnipresent Power. The *Vedas* speak of God in a variety of ways and finally declare: God is *be-anta*.

There comes a stage in life (and this is a process of evolution), when we realise that God is all kindness; He is the source, He is the inspiration; and His grace alone can lead us to true *bhakti*. Then we call out to Him, "O Lord, Thou art infinite. It is Thy kindness that Thou hast come and dwelt in my tiny heart. I regret that I have ignored You, even though You are within me. I have been busy, running after shadow shapes. I have been wasting time in useless activities, in the pursuit of the pleasures of life. My Beloved, how is it that I have never thought about You? Grant me the grace to know You, to love You. I cannot love you with all my heart, for it is too tiny. Let me love you, my Beloved, with your heart."

When we utter these words and we realise that the Supreme Lord is seated within us, then our eyes will be filled with tears of devotion, and we will experience true love and longing for the Lord. *Bhakti* (devotion) comes with the awareness of the Omnipresence of the Supreme Being.

There are two kinds of people: those whose hearts are filled with devotion for the Lord, and those who lack in the spirit of true *bhakti*. It is with the grace of God that man can cultivate devotion. Hence we should pray to God to shower His mercy on us, so that we may be imbued with *bhakti*.

A question is often asked, if God is omnipresent, if He is in every grain of sand, in every blade of grass, if He is in every being, then, how is it that He is invisible? How is it that we do not see Him?

A king once asked a sage, 'You say, God is everywhere. Then how is that I am not able to see Him?

The sage replied, "O King, look at the sun.'

The king did so. He gazed at the sun, but could not look at the sun for more than a moment: the glare was too much for his eyes.

Seeing this, the sage said to the King, "The Sun is only one object of His creation. When you are not able to bear the radiance of just one object of His creation, how would you be able to bear the powerful infinite source of that light?'

We are unable to see God, because He is beyond our sense perception. We are able to see what our eyes see; we are able to hear what our ears hear; we are able to feel what our physical hands and feet can touch. God is beyond and above these finite, limited human senses. This is why we are unable to see God; hear God; and touch God. God transcends the senses, the mind and the intellect.

Yes, we shall be able to experience God, if we turn our senses inward. For this, the practice of silence is necessary. Silence takes us beyond words, thoughts and actions. It reveals to us truths of life, and in that created space, devotion is born. Silence not only heals and rejuvenates us, but communicates to us things which are beyond the grasp of our earthly senses. In silence, it is possible for us to see God, may be even to hear His flute-like voice!

Consciousness is built of 3 layers – the superconscious, the conscious, the sub-conscious.

The superconscious is the seat of our highest aspirations.

It is a reservoir of tremendous powers of the spirit. If only we unlock a fraction of these powers there is nothing we cannot achieve.

Awareness Of God's Love

Psychologists tell us that there are three 'states' experienced by every human being – the waking state, the dreaming state and the sleeping state.

Perhaps psychology stops a little short; for our ancient sages spoke of a fourth state of intense concentration beyond these three – a state of which most of us are unaware. It is a state that cannot be easily achieved without *sadhana* and *abhyasa* – self-discipline and regular practice. Not only is this state – known as *turiya* – extremely rare, but it is also a state of cosmic consciousness. When man attains to this state he contacts the truth of existence.

Turiya literally means the fourth state, the supreme consciousness, as distinct from the other three states: waking, dreaming and dreamless sleep. The fourth state is related to the highest level of our intellect, and actually enables us to become aware of the other three states, which operate at the lower levels of our consciousness.

An American friend once said to me, "Here in the western world, we have three states of awareness which are different from yours: we are asleep, we are awake, or we are watching TV!"

Perhaps westerners are not the only ones; many of us are in complete ignorance of this whole dimension of awareness that exists within us.

Sri Ramana Maharishi tells us something of the different levels of the *samadhi* that we can achieve in the fourth state:

(1) Holding on to reality is *samadhi*.

(2) Holding on to reality with effort is *savikalpa samadhi*.

(3) Merging in reality and remaining unaware of the world is *nirvikalpa samadhi*.

(4) Merging in ignorance and remaining unaware of the world is not *samadhi*, but sleep.

(5) Remaining in the primal, pure natural state without effort is *sahaja nirvikalpa samadhi*.

The Fifth state is the prerogative of realised souls. The state of *samadhi* that aspirants can attain to are of two kinds. One is *savikalpa* (with self-consciousness) and the other is *nirvikalpa* (without self-consciousness). In the first type of *samadhi*, the devotee retains his identity. He has the vision of God, he experiences His being, yet there is duality. The devotee is separate from the God. He also experiences great bliss. But when he comes out of the euphoria of *samadhi*, he goes into silence, for his experience has been beyond the description of words. His experience has been mystical and interior.

On the other hand, in the second type of *samadhi*, the devotee loses his identity. He experiences oneness with the Divine. There is no duality of the devotee and the object of his devotion. The devotee is immersed in the ocean of divinity and within him arises the sublime emotion of divine love for all. It is an extraordinary experience of ecstasy; it is a union with the Divine, it is yoga at its highest state. When Sri Chaitanya went to visit Gaya, he was a professor of Logic. When he returned after visiting Gaya, he was a transformed man. When he returned he was lost in the devotion for Lord Krishna. He was intoxicated with the words, *"Krishna, Krishna, Krishna Bol", "Hari, Hari, Hari, Bol"*. He could see nothing else, but the image of Sri Krishna. He had attained the state of enlightenment, of self-realisation.

Gurudev Sadhu Vaswani often said to us that every man has some obsession or the other. Some are obsessed with money, some with pleasure, some with name, fame and social status. Blessed is the man who is obsessed with *bhakti* for Sri Krishna. Saint Mira in one of her *bhajans*, sings, *"Main to prem diwani"* (I am drenched with Love for Sri Krishna).

But what of us, ordinary mortals? When will we be immersed in that ocean of love?

Once Gurudev Sadhu Vaswani was asked a question, "How may we realise Sri Krishna? Where can we seek Him?"

Sadhu Vaswani's reply was based on his own experience, "Years ago, I had a great yearning to realise Sri Krishna," he said to us. "I went in search of Him. I went to Temples and Gurudwaras. I visited places of pilgrimage. I went to the mountain tops and to the banks of sacred rivers. I had just one yearning: to seek God. There was just one cry in my heart: 'O my Beloved, where art Thou? Where should I seek You? Where should I find You?' And yet I could not find Sri Krishna.

"One day, as the sun went down and twilight spread in the sky, I went and sat under a tree. I wept tears of yearning. My thirst for the Lord increased and I could no longer bear the separation. It was then that I heard a voice. The voice said, 'My dear, I dwell where the poor live. I dwell where the poor and the downtrodden, the lonely, the forlorn and the forsaken are revered and served. For they are my images; they are the pictures of Him whom you seek..'"

Gurudev Sadhu Vaswani, therefore, exhorted us to serve the poor, the sick, the handicapped and the helpless with love and devotion; for, as he said to us repeatedly, "The poor are the pictures of God. To serve them is truly to worship God."

Lord Krishna's love is magical. His love is like *paras* (philosopher's stone), which turns base material into gold. Sri Krishna's love magically transforms the seeker and the devotee is born anew. He has discarded the lower emotions of envy, jealousy and greed. He is fearless and does not worry. He is forever free!

We get ruffled up by the reactions of the people around us. We are paranoid about what people say and think about us. And this binds us to a fear of 'loss of face'.

There was a rich man, whose coffers were filled with gold, silver, precious gems and jewels. Did that make him a happy, contented man, grateful to God for the abundant wealth bestowed on him? Unfortunately, that was not the case! He was always on the lookout for more and more wealth.

One day as he was going through the bazaar, he noticed a tiny sparkling red stone. He thought it was a ruby and so he tried to pick it up from the ground. The sparkling little stone was not a ruby, but a piece of beetle-nut coloured by the red juice of the *paan*. In fact, it had been spat out by a careless *paan* chewer! The tiny piece of the chewed and spat out beetle-nut sparkled like a ruby in the rays of the sun. When the silly, greedy man realised his mistake, he became acutely embarrassed and self-conscious. Afraid of being laughed at and mocked, he threw away the disgusting morsel he had picked up, looked here and there and hoped desperately that no one had seen him, before he made his hasty exit from the place.

This kind of fear is natural with the people who worry about the reactions of others. I have even seen people who fall down, look out anxiously to see if anyone has seen them. Their first reaction is, "Has anyone seen me fall? Is anyone laughing at me?" Such is the extent of our obsession with public opinion – the fear of 'what people will say'.

A few days later, our rich friend was invited to the wedding anniversary celebrations of a neighbour. It was a grand party with entertainers and singers to keep the audience amused. One of the performers looked at the rich man and sang, "I have come to know, I have come to know…"

The rich man was taken aback with unpleasant surprise. He thought to himself, "My God! This girl probably saw me in the bazaar the other day, picking up that disgusting piece of chewed betel nut! Otherwise, why would she stare at me and sing 'I have come to know, I have come to know.' I had better shut her up before she reveals the truth to all."

He took out a hundred rupee note and gave it to the singer. The performer thought that the rich man was pleased with her song, so she sang with further gusto, "I have come to know, I have come to know." The rich man was now worried. He removed his expensive silk shawl and flung it on her shoulders. Encouraged by this generous gesture, the performer raised her voice and sang, "I will tell it all, I will tell it all."

The rich man was flabbergasted. He became paranoid now. He did not want the world to know that he had picked up a dirty chewed up and spat out piece of beetle-nut from the dirty street of the bazaar. As for the performer, she continued to sing, "The time has come to reveal the secret." Unable to bear the turmoil in his mind, the rich man screamed, "What have I done, I only picked up that chewed beetle-nut by mistake!" The performer could not grasp the meaning of his words. But the gathering went into peals of laughter.

We are like that rich man, always afraid, always full of fear and anxiety. A devotee of Lord Krishna, on the other hand, is free of all fear and worry, because he has absolute faith in God.

Superficiality characterises everything we do. We judge people by the clothes they wear and the cars they drive. We occupy our minds with what we would like to eat, what we would like to buy and what we could do to impress friends and neighbours. We have no time to think of the world within!

In our constant state of superficial existence, we continue to ignore the world within. In our persistent chase after shadow-shapes and worldly wealth, we lose sight of our inner consciousness. We emphasise speech, action and outward show; we forget that there is a far more valuable aspect to life called reflection, contemplation, introspection. Men and women of speech and action, there are very many; alas, men and women of reflection and contemplation, there are very few.

A leading practitioner of meditation in the United States once pointed out that several cultures and religions simply do not teach people to focus on the world within them; their emphasis is often on words, rites and rituals; on a form or a Being or Spirit *outside*; thus the innermost spirit remains out of reach of most people.

The Indian tradition on the other hand, has always placed great value on meditation, reflection and contemplation – on the state of inner silence and inner stillness. For it is in this state that we will find tranquillity, serenity, self-knowledge and true awareness. In this state, too, we will experience true freedom – freedom from fears, desires, tensions, insecurities and complexes that haunt us in the waking state. In this state of inner consciousness, we will also discover our own Divinity – that we are not the bodies we wear, we are not the insignificant, pathetic, frail creatures that we take ourselves to be; we will discover that we are the immortal *atman*, the eternal, infinite spirit that is *Sat-chit-ananda* – pure, true, eternal Bliss!

People drink alcohol, so they say, to get intoxicated, to forget their stress and worries. Let us drink, instead, the nectar of Sri Krishna's love and become intoxicated, like Mira, like Chaitanya, like Andal. That is true intoxication. That is true ecstasy. This intoxication comes with the awareness that God loves everyone of us. His love is infinite. His love is beyond description. At every moment, at every step He is with us; He protects us. When we cultivate this awareness, we are unafraid, unperturbed by all that befalls us. We are content to realise that we are in God's hands.

People who do not cultivate this awareness are storm-tossed by fear and worry. Every untoward incident, every unexpected event upsets their balance. They lose faith in God.

There was a woman whose husband had gone abroad on an overseas business. All of a sudden, he fell ill. He contracted typhoid and died there. On getting the news of her husband's death, the woman was distracted beyond reason. She began to blame God. She accused her Guru of not taking care of her.

Is it in our nature to blame someone else for all the evil that befalls us? We rarely stop to examine the truth. We never ever consider our own karmic burdens. For all the illnesses and mishaps in our life, we conveniently choose to blame God. The fact is, whatever is happening to us in this life, is the result of our past karmas. In a way, it is our own doing. God is not to be blamed for it.

To continue with the story of this woman, she had a nine month old child. Forced to care for the child on her own, she left no opportunity to blame God, to accuse Him of cruelty and injustice. One day, carrying the child, she went to the market place. There she came across a holy man; seeing him, she became furious. In her mood of self-righteous indignation, she felt, he was the representative of an unfair, unjust God. She hurled out at him, abusive words about God in general and holy men in particular.

The holy man was not upset. A sensitive and sympathetic soul, he could fathom the pain of this widowed woman left to care for the child. He called her to his side and gently said to her, "My dear sister, throw this child away and I shall give you one thousand Rupees."

The woman was shocked. "Have I heard you right?" she asked. The holy man said, "Throw your child away, for, as you say, he is a terrible burden on you, and it is unfair to expect you to carry this burden on your own. Therefore, I say to you, throw this terrible burden away, and I will give you ten thousand Rupees."

The woman was flabbergasted. "Are you crazy to talk to me like this?"

The holy man said to her, "But, dear sister, it was you who complained that God had inflicted this terrible burden on you! Throw your child away and I will give you one lakh of Rupees. May be, you will feel adequately compensated for God's cruelty to you."

The woman screamed, "Are you in your senses? Are you aware of what you are saying? Do you know how much I love my child? He is the light of my life. How can I throw him away?" The holy man smiled and said, "Just as you love the child, so too, God loves you and your child! He loves all of us. He loves us a thousand times more than you love your child. How can you call Him cruel and blame Him for your misfortunes?"

Once we become aware of God's love, we will develop reverence and devotion for Him. Hinduism teaches us that the easiest way to live life is to love all living things, and thus discover the love of God: for love of our fellow human beings, love for all creation, leads us to love of God.

Conditional love says : I love You, because I need You!
Unconditional love says: I need You because I love You.

Unconditional Love

What is *Bhakti*? More than anything else, *bhakti* is deep love, for the One and only Beloved, a love which, in due course, moves out to all. Such deep devotion, such universal love does not come easily to us because we are groping in the darkness of ignorance. We are trapped in the *maya* of this world. It is because of this veil of ignorance that we equate all worldly pleasures with true happiness and joy. In reality there is no pleasure without pain.

We are prisoners of desires. Every desire carries a seed of sorrow, a seed of pain and disillusion. We tend to consider the truth as untruth and untruth as truth. We tend to consider the finite as infinite and the limited as unlimited. Running after the shadow shapes of life, we get exhausted and break down. When man experiences even an iota of Divine Love, a deep devotion rises within him. His yearning for the Lord is awakened and he calls out, "O Lord, I need Thee, and Thee alone!"

In the terrible *Kalyug* that we are passing through, man is in the grip of desire, illusion and arrogance.

At such times, the easiest and surest way to attain to God is the way of devotion – *Bhakti Marga*. Saints and holy men tell us that the way of *Bhakti* is the way of surrender. There are many other ways to reach God – the way of *karma,* the way of *gnana*. But these are not accessible to us all. In the days of *Kalyug,* man is so lost in worry and anxiety; he carries a heavy burden of grief upon his heart. For such a one, the way of devotion is easiest and most simple.

What are the marks of true *bhakti*? The first mark is self surrender. A man of devotion surrenders totally to the Lord. In this self surrender lies the devotion which is selfless. This love is pure and universal. It is given to one and all, without any distinction. The second mark is fearlessness. A man of *bhakti* is free from fear. Many devotees pray to God and worship Him out of fear. They do not want to incur either His displeasure or His wrath. Hence, they appeal to Him for protection and care. They please Him with offerings of all kinds. But, a man of *bhakti* loves God out of the deepest emotions of his heart. He does not plead either for protection or safety. Such a man knows that God is the protector of us all, and whatever He does is just right for us.

Many people grope in the darkness of fear and ignorance and take refuge in rituals, equating rituals with devotion. They find solace, nay, relief from worry and anxiety in performing *puja* and other rituals. There was once a woman who religiously performed

Satyanarayan Puja on the Full Moon day of every month. She fasted on that day and offered her prayers. Once, just once, she forgot to fast and offer prayers. She was dismayed when she realised her oversight; she felt that God would be displeased, angered by this act. Sure enough, her husband contracted an illness soon thereafter. "God is punishing me," she thought desperately. "I failed to observe the *vrat* I was committed to, and I am being punished for it."

She did not once pause to think: how can God ever think of punishing us? God is above all our earthly limitations. How can the Divine Power ever be displeased? God is our Mother and God is our Father. How can He misunderstand us?

However, this woman felt sure that God was unhappy with her, because she failed to fast on the Full Moon day and that is why her husband had fallen ill.

The husband would have fallen ill anyway. His illness had no relevance to the non-observation of the *Satyanarayan Puja*.

I often find that people are reluctant to surrender to God. They are ashamed, nay, reluctant, to seek refuge at His Holy Feet. They feel that they are impure, unworthy of His love. They think: we have committed so many sins, how will God ever accept us? What they fail to realise is that God is like a loving Mother, who will pick up Her dirty, naughty child, and clean them up thoroughly. God will cleanse us of our filth, our sins and misdeeds and embrace us with love, even as a mother does. God is above good and evil. Perhaps, when we understand this, it will free us from fear.

Where there is fear, there can be no *bhakti*. *Bhakti* is not expressed through rituals, nor is it a form of 'bribe' we offer to God, for protecting us from harm. *Bhakti* is like the bird that sings soulfully in the garden of God. Its song is not dependent on who is watching, or who is listening; nor does it sing out of fear or favour. It just sings, because the song conveys its joy. Our *bhakti*, too, should be spontaneous, like the birdsong.

Bhakti has two wings, even as a bird takes flight on its two wings. The first is thirst, the second is humility.

Na ham, na ham, tu ho, tu ho!

I am naught. Thou alone art!

It is but a thin veil that separates us from the Lord; this is the veil of the ego, of arrogance; of pride. When this veil drops, we will behold the face of the Beloved.

Have you ever shed tears for the love of the Lord? If you haven't, you cannot experience the bliss of loving Him.

What do tears have to do with love, you may ask.

Have you seen how children cry when their mother leaves them for one reason or the other? It is not that they cry because they are unhappy — they cry because they love their mother so much that they cannot bear to be parted from her.

We must realise that we too, are children who have been separated from our Divine Mother. We have become separated from God, our true Beloved. Alas, this is a truth that very few of us are aware of — that we are in a state of separation from the Beloved. When this realisation dawns on us, we begin to shed tears.

Most of us are so caught up in the entanglements of this world. We are so enslaved by what the world has given us — pleasure, possessions and power — that we do not even feel the need for God. How then can we shed tears for Him?

It is only after much wandering that this realisation dawns on man — that he is living a life of separation from God. He may then begin to feel that his wandering has taken him so far away from God — and this will bring tears to His eyes.

It is then that he decides that he must begin his journey *back* to God, for this is the only journey that will make his life worthwhile. When he embarks on this journey, out of the depths of his heart will arise the cry: "Beloved, take the wanderer Home!" and the tears begin to flow... tears of thirst for the Lord.

Rabia was once asked, "How do you worship God? Do you wait for God to enter your consciousness and then begin your prayer? Or is it the other way round

– you begin your prayer and then God enters your heart?"

Rabia replied, "I do neither of these things. When my eyes are moist, when tears of love and longing flow from my eyes, I see God before me."

Thirst, yearning, profound longing for the Lord, is the first step on the *bhakti marga*.

Utter humility is the second step, the ability to conquer arrogance and pride and rise above the ego.

A *satsangi* brother once said to me "Many are the valuable lessons and morals that I have absorbed from the daily *satsang*. But there is one truth that has impressed me the most and that is – he that is down, need fear no fall." Nothing can bring down the man who bows low in humility. The man, who is high in arrogance and pride, is always threatened by downfall. Therefore let us all aspire to the virtue of humility.

Pride is a man's worst enemy. Pride is what we associate with Ravana. Two major vices brought about Ravana's downfall – the first was that he was arrogant; the second was that he was addicted to sensual pleasures. Alas, it is these two vices that now enslave all humanity. What we see all around us in the world today is Ravana *Raj* – the rule of Ravana. It is only Lord Rama who can save us from its evil. When we are blessed with the Lord's grace, the realisation dawns on each one of us: I am nothing, the Lord is all. *Naham, naham, tu ho, tu ho!* The man who attains this realisation conquers his desires and passions and follows the path of *sadhana*.

A wealthy merchant was crossing the market place when a beggar approached him. "Take pity on me," begged the poor man. "There is not a grain of food with me, and my wife and children have been starving for three days. In vain have I looked for work so that I may earn enough to feed them. But I have not found employment. The Lord in his mercy has blessed you with abundant wealth. Take pity on me and help me out of your munificence and generosity!"

"Get lost," said the merchant in his pride and arrogance." You will not get a paisa out of me."

The Lord tells Arjuna in the *Bhagavad Gita* that it is He who dwells in every living creature. Therefore, when we hurt any living thing, we actually hurt the Lord Himself. The wealthy merchant was not aware that he insulted the Lord when he spoke harsh words to the beggar.

"Have mercy on me," entreated the beggar. "Give me something to feed my family, or we shall all die of hunger."

Infuriated, the merchant cried out in anger, "Get out of here, you rascal! Get out, I say!"

Just a little wealth can make man so proud and arrogant! When the poor man began his entreaties again the merchant was so incensed that he slapped the beggar. The poor man was so weak and emaciated that he fell under his blows. Thus it is, that in the pride of wealth and power, we exploit the weak and the helpless.

I said to you earlier that many of us remain trapped in the entanglements of the world. This is true of every *sansari jeeva* – he is intoxicated with the pleasures, possessions and powers of this world. He is intoxicated with worldly love and longing – with *I, Me* and *Mine*.

He must detoxify himself of this *maya* and enter into another kind of intoxication – he must lose himself, nay, drown himself in the intoxication of God's love. Such a one will find himself shedding unbidden tears of love and longing for the Lord. Such tears are like the clean and pure Ganga that fell from Heaven, as a result of Bhagiratha's *tapasya*. This Ganga will purify you, cleanse you and put you in the right frame of mind. In this state you will feel that God is not from you afar. He does not dwell in a far-off temple. You do not have to go to a *tapovan* (forest of meditation) or a mountain-peak to find Him. He is *here* – He is *now* – He is in the heart within you. You can speak to Him, commune with Him as with a friend or with a member of your own family. Establish contact with Him in silence – and be prepared to LISTEN – for in the depths of silence will you hear His divine voice, not in the clamour and noise of this world.

The *Narada Bhakti Sutras* speaks of eleven different components, or eleven different aspects of *bhakti*: such as adoration of the Lord's quality (*Guna*), His form (*Rupa*), His *Puja* (ritual), meditation on Him (*Smarana*) etc. But it talks also about five different *bhakti bhavas* or attitudes. These are:

1. *Santa bhava* – in this attitude the devotee is at peace. He is not emotional. He does not shed tears, or weep or sing or dance in ecstasy. Yet his heart is full of intense devotion. We may cite Bhishama Pitamaha as a wonderful example of this attitude – for he adored the Lord without any outer form of expression. In modern times, Sri Aurobindo too exemplified this aspect. Many renunciates (*sanyasis*) have this attitude.

2. *Madhurya bhava* – in this, the devotee loves the Lord even as a lover adores his beloved. Even today, in Mathura, Brindaban and Nadiad, you will find devotees with this attitude. The *Ashtapadi* of Jayadev captures this attitude beautifully, dwelling on the *ras-leela* of Radha and Krishna.

3. *Sakhya bhava* – in which the devotee sees himself as the Lord's companion.

4. *Vatsalya bhava* – in which the devotee loves God as her own child. This attitude is unique to the Indian *bhakt* tradition. The saints and Alwars imagine themselves to be Ma Yashoda, holding Sri Krishna in her arms, even while she enjoys His divine *leela*.

5. *Dasya bhava* – in which the devotee regards himself as a servant to the Lord, who is his Master.

This should teach us that we must approach God in the form that appeals most to us: make Him your friend; make Him your loving parent; make Him your Beloved. In whatever form you approach Him, He will gladly respond to you!

So far, I have spoken to you of spontaneous *bhakti*; but aspirants on the path may also cultivate *bhakti* through *sadhana*. Our sages have identified different stages by which one may attain *Bhakti*. This requires certain spiritual practises.

1. *Shravana* – listening. For the aspirant, *satsang* is vital, because it enables us to listen to the voice of the enlightened ones, to readings from scriptures. Listening to *satvishaya* (good teachings) repeatedly, sets us on the spiritual path easily.

2. *Kirtana* – (singing) is the next step. I have always maintained that singing the Name Divine is the shortest route to God. Chaitanya Mahaprabhu was a great exponent of this practise.

3. *Smarana* – (constant remembrance) of the Lord is the next step. In this stage, we become aware of the Divine presence in everything we see, we hear, we do or we say; we feel His presence in every breath we take. Our life is enfolded in His presence.

4. *Archana* – (offering flowers) is not just a ritual. Symbolically, it implies that we offer good qualities, virtues like humility, compassion and goodness to the Lord.

5. *Padasevana* – (serving the feet) symbolises the spirit of service. This is what Gurudev Sadhu Vaswani

meant, when he described service of the poor as the best form of worship to God.

6. *Vandana* – (bowing down) within the heart, the devotee reveres the Lord; outwardly, he reveres all creatures, all objects which are, after all, manifestations of the Divine.

7. *Atmanivedana* – is absolute surrender. This is the ultimate goal of spiritual attainment – to live in total surrender to the Lord. *Bhakti yoga,* the path of devotion to the Lord, is in essence, the path of love – love that is unconditional, whole-hearted, selfless and completely fulfilling. Alas, human love is frittered away on worldly objects and goals that are perishable, mortal and therefore, utterly futile. But when our love is bestowed on God, we find complete and absolute fulfilment. We transcend the ego, and commune with the Divine. We seek to find our self ultimately reflected in the Divine Self. This is the perfect object of love that we have been seeking through several embodiments, several births. In *bhakti yoga*, this sublime attainment is reached in the highest state of complete and utter surrender. Each step that you take towards this goal is blessed; for it has truly been said that the person who grows in the spirit of *bhakti* does good not only to himself, but to all humanity.

Repetition of the Name Divine is the most effective remedy for all the ills of life. It is a potent pep-pill that will lift you out of depression and exhaustion.

The Magic Of The Name Divine

Can God take a human birth? The rational western mind does not accept this proposition. But, we of the Hindu faith, believe that God does take a human form, time and again, for the salvation of mankind. In the Srimad Bhagavad Gita, Lord Krishna says:

> *yada yada hi dharmasya*
> *glanir bhavati bharata*
> *abhyutthanam adharmasya*
> *tadatmanam srjamyaham*
>
> *paritranaaya saadhunaam*
> *vinashaya cha dushkritam*
> *dharma samstaapanaartha*
> *sambhavaami yuge yuge...*

Whenever and wherever there is decline of *dharma* (righteousness) and ascendance of *adharma* (unrighteousness), at that time I manifest Myself in visible form. For the protection of the righteous and destruction of the wicked, and for the sake of establishing *dharma* again, I incarnate Myself on earth age after age.

Prayer cleanses your thoughts, purifies your mind and elevates your consciousness.

That is the Lord's promise to us!

During the *Tretayuga*, Lord Vishnu came to this earth in the form of Sri Rama. He was born as the heir to the Raghukul dynasty, the eldest son of King Dasharatha of Ayodhya. People may dismiss the 'Theory of Incarnation', as they call it, but every believing Hindu will assure you, that it is indeed true that Sri Rama was the incarnation of Lord Vishnu. The evidence of our sacred *puranas* corroborates this.

Why should God come to earth in a human form, ask the 'rationalists' and non-believers. I don't think this is to be dismissed as improbable or impossible, because God is our Father in Heaven; He is the One Who created us and protects us here upon this earth: why would he not take birth on earth in order to guard us and defend us from the utter darkness of *adharma*? People of other faiths do not give credence to the 'Theory of Incarnation' of God.

To give you an amusing anecdote in this regard, let me tell you of King Akbar and his minister Birbal, who once had a conversation on this topic. King Akbar observed, rather mockingly, "You Hindus are funny people. You say God Himself takes human birth and appears on this earth. Tell me, why would the Supreme take a human form and appear on this wretched earth? Surely He has the power to accomplish whatever he wishes without actually coming down here in human form."

To this Birbal replied, "Your Highness, there is nothing strange in this. God is our Father, so why would He not come on this earth to protect us, if the need arises?" Akbar could not take the argument further. He burst out laughing, dismissing the conversation.

A few days later, Akbar asked Birbal to go for a walk with him, along the river bank. As they were strolling, Emperor Akbar saw a boat caught in the vortex of swirling waters. He also saw that the woman sitting in the boat was a servant from his palace – in fact, she was none other than his child's *ayah*. She was screaming, as she held a small baby in her arms. Emperor Akbar naturally jumped to the conclusion that the child was his own son. As he watched in horror, the boat rocked dangerously, and the babe in the *ayah's* hands slipped and fell into the swirling waters. Without a moment's thought, Akbar jumped into the water and with a tremendous feat of courage, reached the drowning child and retrieved him. It was only then that he realised that the 'baby' was just a wooden doll.

As for Birbal, he stood on the river bank, watching the whole drama unfold, with an amused smile. When Akbar swam back to the shore, crestfallen and panting from the unexpected exertion, Birbal gave him a helping hand to climb out on to the shore. When the king had been towelled dry by shocked assistants who simply did not understand what was happening, Birbal said to him, "O mighty Emperor, you are surrounded by dozens of guards and servants, as well as faithful courtiers like me. Yet, when you thought your child was in danger, you did not order anyone of us to jump in the river and save him. You were a father first and foremost. Without waiting for a moment you rushed to save your child. It is the same with God, our Father in Heaven. Whenever He finds that humanity has reached its brink, He takes the form of a human being and becomes the saviour of mankind."

As I said earlier, Sri Rama was the incarnation of Lord Vishnu. King Dasharatha had in all, four sons – Sri Rama, Lakshmana, Bharata and Shatrugna. It was Sri Rama, who, right from his childhood had radiated a tremendous spiritual energy. The *rishis* of that age were aware of the supreme power, the omnipotence of Sri Rama. The epic Ramayana narrates an incident which shows us this power.

In those days, the *rishis* used to sit in *tapasya* in the forests, offering *yagnas* to appease the Lord. The Vedas enjoin all *rishis* to offer such sacrifices. It was thought that all mankind derived the benefit of these *yagnas*, for they were meant for human welfare and the preservation of *dharma*.

Often, demons would disturb them in their meditation or spoil their *yagna* offerings, by throwing in pieces of flesh and other pollutants into the sacred *havan* fire. Even the *rishis* could not be spared from the evil energies of demonic beings. Tired of the mischief played by the evil forces, Rishi Vishwamitra, the leader of the *tapasvis,* went to King Dasharatha. He said to him, "O King, you are our ruler and our protector. We are tired of enduring the tyranny of the evil forces. Please do your duty and protect us from the demons. Send your child Rama with us; we shall take him with us to the *tapobana,* the forest of meditation. We are convinced that he alone can vanquish the demons."

Sri Rama was a small boy at that time. His father was quite alarmed by Sage Vishwamitra's demand. He wondered how this small child would fight the dark demons. So he offered instead, his army along with weapons and the services of his commanders. But Rishi Vishwamitra, who could see the divine strength of Sri Rama, rejected the offer and insisted on taking Sri Rama alone. In his moments of yogic communion with the Divine, he had been told that it was only Sri Rama who could conquer the demons. Helpless, not wishing to offend the *rishi,* Dasharatha permitted Sri Rama to go with him. Lakshmana also accompanied him, for the brothers were inseparable. Lakshmana too, for his part, was positive about Sri Rama's supreme power. He knew that he and his brother were on a winning mission.

As we know, Sri Rama and Lakshmana destroyed the demons who were disturbing the *yagnas* of the *rishis.* On their way back to Ayodhya, Rishi Vishwamitra took them to Mithila, where Sita's *Swayamwar* was being held. (This is an ancient tradition whereby a girl could choose her bridegroom at her own discretion). One of the conditions for selecting the bridegroom was, that he should pick up and string the *Rudhra danush* – the bow of Lord Shiva, which had been gifted to her father, King Janaka. Sri Rama participated in the *Swayamwar*, at the instance of his Guru, Rishi Vishwamitra. There were many aspirant bridegrooms, all of them famous kings and princes, but none of them could even lift the bow, leave alone hold it and string it. Sri Rama not only picked up the bow effortlessly, but strung it so powerfully, that the mighty bow actually broke in his hands. Delighted, Sita chose Sri Rama as her husband, with the blessings of her father.

Let me remind you of another episode from the Ramayana, which demonstrates Sri Rama's extraordinary spiritual power. It is of course, a beloved, well known story, but who can tire of hearing it repeatedly? The more we hear of the Lord and His *leela*, the more we are blessed!

Sri Rama is preparing for his coronation as *Yuvaraj* of Ayodhya. Early in the morning on the appointed day, when he has bathed in sanctified waters, and dressed in his new, silken royal robes, he is summoned to go to his father, King Dasharatha. As he rides in his princely chariot, he sees the city radiant with joy and celebration; the people cheer him on his way, assuming that the holy rituals of the coronation are about to begin.

Alas, reality is different. Sri Rama is told by Kaikeyi that he must give up his right to the throne and go into the forest as an exile — for fourteen long years. It is a boon that she has received from King Dasharata, and as a son, it is Rama's duty to help his father keep the promise he has made.

Sri Rama — the *maryada purushottam* or ideal man that he was, did not so much as flinch! We are told by Rishi Valmiki, that when he left Kaikeyi's palace, he did not ride in his chariot — for mentally, he had already renounced his royal life!

Did he not have provocation enough to rage and protest? Why, when Lakshmana heard the news, his anger was uncontrollable! When Bharata returned from his trip, he was so incensed by his mother's deed that he cursed her and turned his back upon her for making him the pretext of her terrible scheme!

But Sri Rama remained unperturbed, calm, unmoved — the *Stitha Prajna*. What a glorious example for us to cherish!

Sri Rama during his period of banishment fights the dark forces, banishes the threat of evil and *adharma*, and brings peace to the forest regions of *Bharat varsha*. As we know, Ravana takes away Sita from her *kutiya*, in the forest. He changes his form to appear as a mendicant, and ensnares Sita in his evil design. Sri

Rama now has to cross the ocean and go to Lanka to rescue His beloved Sita.

The question now arises, how did Sri Rama manage to cross the ocean in order to go to Lanka? It is said, that Sri Rama with the help of Sugreeva and his army of *vanaras*, built a *setu* (bridge) across the waters of the southern sea, a geographical wonder that can still be seen in our latest satellite images, and which devout Hindus regard as a place of sacred pilgrimage – the *Rama Setu* near Danushkoti.

How was this marvellous structure constructed? The army of monkeys picked up heavy stones and inscribed the Name of 'Rama' on each one. When they threw these stones in the water, they floated. It was nothing but a divine miracle. As the *setu* was being built, Sri Rama felt that it was time to tell the world something about the Power of the Name Divine. He picked up a huge stone and threw it in the water, but the stone sank. The army of monkeys were surprised. Sri Rama explained, "The stones thrown by you with the Name 'Rama' floated because they had the power of the Name; but the stone I threw sank. The moral of this is, that the Name of Sri Rama is more powerful than Sri Rama himself."

Guru Nanak in his sacred verse tells us, "*Vada Sahib, Oocha Thaon, Oonche Upar Ooncha Nao.*" The Name of God is the *Alpha*, the highest. There is nothing higher than that. Hence, say the beads of the Name Divine with every breath of your life. Fortunate is the man who understands the divinity of the word, 'Rama'. Such a man lives in the world but never ever forgets the Name Divine. The chanting of the sacred word goes on within his heart. The Name of 'Rama' is so sacred that by chanting it man can overcome his desires. He can raise his energy from the lower *chakras* to the higher *chakras*. Chanting the Name Divine gives him spiritual strength.

Sri Rama's incarnation as a King of Ayodhya and his varied experiences are a lesson for humanity. The Name of Sri Rama is exalted by saints and sages alike. The sacred Guru Granth Sahib also venerates the Name of Sri Rama and so does Kabir Granth. Gurudev Sadhu Vaswani too venerated the Name of Sri Rama in the Nuri Granth. It would be no exaggeration to say that the Name of Sri Rama is inscribed on the soul of India.

We too repeat the Name 'Rama' but some of us do so without any meaning. By merely uttering the Name 'Rama', with our lips no benefit can be accrued. It will give us the maximum benefit, when we utter the Name with true reverence and devotion that comes from within.

The Name 'Rama' is made up of two words, 'Ra' and 'Ma'. It is said that the essence of *"Om Namoh Narayana"* is in 'Ra' and the essence of *"Om Namah Shivai"* is in 'Ma'. The two together form, 'Rama'. In other words 'Rama' has the power and divinity of both the sacred mantras, *"Om Namoh Narayana"* and *"Om Namah Shivai"*.

In one of the *puranas*, we come across an instance where the deities began to fight among themselves. The issue of the quarrel was: who is the most powerful deity? Every deity blew his own trumpet, highlighting his *shakti*. The matter could not be settled because each one was trying to be one up on the other!

It was finally decided that all the deities would request Lord Brahma, to act as their judge and referee. "It is you who must tell us who is the superior one amongst us," they told him.

Brahma replied, "To know who is superior among you, you all will have to go through a test. I do not want to favour anyone or recommend anyone. Hence, your own actions will prove your superiority." Brahma then specified the 'event' in which all of them would have to compete: this was to take a full round or circumambulation of the planet earth; whosoever finished first would be declared as superior.

All the deities rushed to go round the earth. As you know, each deity has his own vehicle, according to the *puranas*. Lord Ganesh mounted his mouse, but was unable to start the journey. Wise as He was, He sought the help of Maharishi Narada. Naradmuni, as we all know, is the one who creates all the riddles and enigmas and he is also the one who solves them. Naradmuni said to Ganesh, "It does not matter. Just write the word 'Rama' and go round it. The entire universe is encompassed in the word 'Rama'." Lord Ganesh did so and was the first one to reach Brahma.

Brahma was amazed. He asked Ganesh, "Did you not go around the earth?" Ganesh replied, "I have taken the round of the earth and returned." Brahma expressed his surprise; "So soon...?", he said, in disbelief. Lord Ganesh then spoke of the word 'Rama' and said that he circumambulated the word 'Rama', which contained the entire universe in it. Brahma accepted the argument of Ganesh and declared Lord Ganesh as the Superior Deity of all deities. That is why, Lord Ganesh is considered as a good omen. Even today, every worship, every *puja* offered in our homes and temples begins with the praise of Lord Ganesh. He knew the greatness of the word 'Rama'.

Once Lord Shiva and his consort Parvati were sitting on Mount Kailash. It was mid-noon. Parvati Devi had brought meals for Lord Shiva. Seeing just one plate of food, Lord Shiva says to Parvati, "My beloved, everyday you bring two plates of food and we eat our meals together. Today, you have brought only one plate; why is this so?"

Parvati Devi replied, "Today I was busy since morning and had no time to chant the sacred *mantra* of Lord Vishnu. Hence, I will first pray and have my meals later." To this Lord Shiva replied, "I will share a secret with you. All the chants are encompassed in the word 'Rama'. So if you just chant the Name of 'Rama' even once, you would have completed your schedule of incantation of the entire Vishnu *sahasranama*, or the thousand names of Vishnu!"

There are many instances of miracles performed with the word 'Rama'. Let me tell you about one from the life of Sant Kabir. Once, a leper-beggar went to his house to get his blessings. Sant Kabir was not at home at that time. The leper knocked on the door and asked to see Sant Kabir. Sant Kabir's wife, Loi, opened the door.

The leper asked her, "Where is Sant Kabir?"

Loi asked the leper, "What is your problem?" The leper replied, "I am suffering from the deadly disease of leprosy and I was told that if I have a glimpse of Sant Kabir, I would be cured of my disease."

Loi replied, "Sant Kabir has gone out. But it is not difficult to cure you of your illness. If you would chant with me, the Divine Name of 'Rama' you would be free from the disease." Loi began to recite the Name of 'Rama' and the leper repeated after her. This was done three times. Three times Loi repeated the name 'Rama' and the leper followed. As he chanted the name of 'Rama' his disease receded and in no time he was completely cured. Pleased with the miracle, the beggar left in a hurry without even waiting to thank Sant Kabir.

On Sant Kabir's return Loi narrated the incident to him. Sant Kabir said, "Where was the need to chant the Name of 'Rama' three times? Once would have been sufficient!"

To this Loi replied, "It is true. With the very first utterance of the Name 'Rama' the man was cured. But I could visualise that this man would get the same disease in his next two births and so I thought to myself, why not relieve him from his suffering of the next two births right away."

Such is the power of the word 'Rama'.

Utter the Name 'Rama' with devotion and you will be cleansed of all evils.

Once there lived a woman of ill-repute. Her name was Jaywanti but in her business she was known as Ganka. As she was all alone and had no one for company, she kept a caged parrot as her pet. She had taught the parrot to say, 'Rama'. The parrot, as was his habit, would repeat the Name 'Rama' again and again and this woman would also stand by the cage and reply, 'Rama', 'Rama'.

Jaywanti and her pet parrot died at the same time. The messengers of death came to claim them. On one side, were the messengers of darkness and on the other, there were messengers from the Realm of Light. Both put their claim on the woman and her pet. The messengers from darkness said, "She was a woman of ill-repute. She was sinful and we shall take her with us." On the other hand, the messengers of Light said, "In her last breath she uttered the Name 'Rama' and so we shall take her with us to the Realm of Light."

A quarrel ensued between the messengers of both the sides. Ultimately, the messengers of Light defeated the messengers of the dark and took the woman and her pet parrot with them. The messengers of death complained to Yamraaj, the Lord of death. "How is it possible that a woman of ill-repute should go to Heaven?" To this the Lord of Death replied, "Remember, if anyone in his last moment before death so much as utters the word 'Rama' his life is cleansed of all sin and evil deeds."

I urge you to remember the message of this discourse: chant the Name of 'Rama' at all times. It is not easy to call upon the Lord at the time of death. Therefore, utter the Name now, when you are young and fit and healthy, in the full enjoyment of your life. This requires constant practise and effort. The Name 'Rama' is Divine, it is sweeter than honey, it is sweeter than nectar. Just chant the Name 'Rama' and experience its divinity and be ever blessed with Supreme bliss!